CONTENTS

D0334194

Dr Johnson once said that what is learned without inclination is soon forgotten. I think I have provided the inclination by including 350 jokes and 130 aphorisms/anecdotes in the exercises and examples. Sixty illustrations reinforce the lessons. Twenty-five of these are in the form of humorous cartoons, and thirty are actually constructed from the punctuation marks themselves – a feature never before attempted in any book.

The exercises are carefully graded in order of difficulty, ranging from simple questions that every pupil can answer, to some that are useful at examination level. The format of one or two pages per subject, makes the work suitable for use as a homework textbook.

Words vanish from the language, but being replaced by others, their loss is not greatly felt; punctuation marks, however, are strictly limited in number, and are irreplaceable. The colon and the semi-colon – rarely used – are becoming 'endangered species'. I think I have made them easier to understand and use. With many students, the use of the paragraph has become largely a matter of guesswork; the substantial section on the paragraph should go some way to remedy this.

The lessons cover every aspect of punctuation, and are intended to encourage progress from spontaneity of expression, to lucid, constructive writing. That has been my purpose. A minor aim (I hope I have been successful) has been to make it enjoyable at the same time.

John Davis

Also by this author:

Handling Language 1
Handling Language 2
Handling Spelling

HANDLING PUNCTUATION

JOHN DAVIS

Illustrations by John Davis

Stanley Thornes (Publishers) Ltd

To my wife, Renée

First published in 1985 by Hutchinson Education
Reprinted 1988, 1989

Reprinted 1991 by
Stanley Thornes (Publishers) Ltd
Old Station Drive
Leckhampton
CHELTENHAM GL53 0DN
England

British Library Cataloguing in Publication Data

Davis, John, 1921—
    Handling punctuation.
    1. English language—Punctuation
    1. Title
    421   PE1450

    ISBN 0 7487 1017 5

Typeset by Words & Pictures Ltd, Thornton Heath, Surrey
Printed and bound in Great Britain by Martin's of Berwick

THE FULL STOP THAT ENDS THE SENTENCE

ALL PUNCTUATION MARKS HAVE VALUE, BUT THE PEARL BEYOND PRICE IS THE FULL STOP.

FULL STOP

SENTENCE
SENTENCE
SENTENCE

A sentence makes complete sense. It begins with a capital letter and it ends with a full stop.

The full stop is the most important punctuation mark because we write in sentences, or statements. Without full stops, a reader would not know where one statement ended and another began. Full stops provide order and meaning.

A If you are not certain that what you have written is a sentence, read it aloud; your ear will tell you if it makes sense, and will correct what your eye may have missed. Read aloud the following item.

The victim was found lying on the floor with a bullet in his chest. <u>A knife sticking out of his back. And a tight rope pulled round his throat</u>. The police suspect foul play.

The parts underlined are not sentences because they do not make complete sense. Here is the correct item:

The victim was found lying on the floor with a bullet in his chest, a knife sticking out of his back, and a tight rope pulled round his throat. The police suspect foul play.

B Write out the following, separating the items into sentences.

1 I know what class hatred is class hatred is when a boy hates everyone else in his class.
2 The bees are on strike they want shorter flowers and more honey.
3 Always borrow money from a pessimist the poor chap doesn't expect to be paid back.
4 There are three ways to get a job done you can do the job yourself, or pay someone to do the job for you the third way is to tell your children that they must not do it.
5 The Ark was being tossed about by a violent storm Noah said to his wife, 'This time, I fear the worst the two rats have just left the ship.'
6 There was a notice in a petshop window: 'Five puppies offered free of charge mother is a pedigree Labrador father is a small brown and white dog capable of climbing a five-foot fence.'
7 7.30 a.m. Open University programme (Science): the planet Earth ends at 8.15 a.m.

Early one morning, in the jungle, I shot an elephant in my pyjamas. How he got into my pyjamas, I shall never know.

THE FULL STOP THAT ENDS THE SENTENCE

A Write out the following, separating the items into sentences.

1 'Once upon a time there was a donkey this donkey lived in a field by the side of a river on the other side of the river there was another field full of delicious carrots the donkey wanted the carrots but the river was too deep for him to wade across it was too wide for him to swim across there was no bridge and he did not have a boat how did he get across the river?'
'I give up.'
'So did the donkey!'

2 'There are three Red Indian women sitting outside their wigwams the first is an average-sized lady, weighing 110 lb she is sitting on a goat-skin the second is a large lady weighing 180 lb she is sitting on a deer-skin the third is an extremely large lady weighing 290 lb her husband has imported a huge hippopotamus hide for her to sit on tell me what this proves.'
'Here is the answer it proves that the squaw on the hippopotamus is equal to the squaw on the other two hides.'

3 A man was rushed to hospital after a snake bit him on the finger doctors removed the poison, saved the finger, and told him to stick it in an ice-pack two weeks later the finger had to be amputated because of frostbite.

4 A friend of mine, who wears a glass eye owing to a wartime injury, recently had to give a lecture as part of an army training course while speaking he rubbed the glass eye, which fell out and dropped onto the floor he pocketed it casually and finished his lecture later, he read his instructor's report: 'Good lecturer, but inclined to let his eye wander.'

B The following sentences have been put in the wrong order. Write them out in the correct sequence as in the drawings below.

Immediately below, was a haystack. Fortunately, he missed the pitchfork. A man fell out of an aeroplane. Unfortunately, he missed the haystack. He was very high up in the sky. In the haystack was a pitchfork.

THE JOINING WORD THAT ACTS LIKE A FULL STOP

Full stops give the reader a chance to 'take a breath' and make sense of each complete sentence. If you use joining words instead of full stops, it is harder for the reader to understand what you are trying to say.

The following has three sentences wrongly joined together:

He can't act and he can't sing and he can dance a little and I asked him his name and he said he was Fred Astaire.

Two of the joining words have been used correctly, and two incorrectly. There should be three sentences, as set out below.

Sentence No. 1:
He can't act and he can't sing.
Sentence No. 2:
He can dance a little.
Sentence No. 3:
I asked him his name, and he said he was Fred Astaire.

A Write out the following in four sentences, by leaving out three of the 'and' joining words.

1 A big theatre once had a Charlie Chaplin Contest and the person who managed to look most like Charlie was to receive a silver cup, and there were other awards for the runners-up and Charlie Chaplin himself decided to enter the contest for fun and he came in second.

B Write out the following in sentences, leaving out all the joining words used incorrectly.

1 'Attention all passengers, this is your Pilot speaking. If you look out at the port engine you will see it is on fire then if you look out at the starboard engine you will see it isn't there and then if you look out and down, you will see a small rubber dinghy in the water and that is where I am speaking from.'

2 There once was a lady trapped with her baby on the roof of a burning building and there was a fireman at the bottom of the building and so he shouted to her: 'Throw down your baby and I will catch him!' and the lady would not do this and then the fireman yelled: 'I am one of the best goalkeepers in the country.' and so the lady threw down her baby and then the fireman caught it, bounced it twice, and then kicked it over a wall.'

THE COMMA THAT DRESSES UP AS A FULL STOP

'That comma thinks he can do our job! Let's grab him and take him before the Judge!'

Because there is a pause after a comma, some people wrongly use a comma instead of a full stop. Avoid this mistake! A comma is simply not able to end a sentence.

Sometimes the mistake happens when a noun ends a sentence, and another noun comes next, bringing with it a new sentence. For example:

1 I have written an unusual murder story. (The word 'story' is a noun, or naming word.)
2 The victim gets killed by a man from another book. (The word 'victim' is also a noun, but there is nothing to connect it with 'murder story', and so it begins a new sentence.)

In most cases, the mistake of using a comma instead of a full stop happens when a noun at the end of a sentence is followed by a pronoun bringing with it a new sentence. For example:

1 Please do not shoot the pianist. (The word 'pianist' is a noun.)
2 He is only doing his best. (The word 'he' is a pronoun, standing in place of the word 'pianist'. It must begin a new sentence, because it is telling something new about the pianist.)

Study the following passage. The last word of each sentence is followed by (NOUN); the first word of the next sentence is followed by (NOUN) or by (PRONOUN).

'Smith' started out as a good old Saxon name from the Old English word 'smid' (NOUN). This (PRONOUN) meant 'smite' and was used to describe anyone who hammered metal on an anvil (NOUN). The name (NOUN) came directly from the blacksmith (NOUN). His (PRONOUN) was a very important and highly respected craft (NOUN). It (PRONOUN) was vital, not only for making farm tools, but also for weapons of war.

Write out the following, changing the commas used wrongly, into full stops.

Three young bulls were standing in a field discussing what they wanted to be when they grew up, the first bull said he wanted to go to Rome and be a papal bull, the second said he wanted to go to Staffordshire and be a bull in a china shop, the third said he just wanted to stay in the pasture for heifer and heifer and heifer.

A cannibal went to see a <u>psychiatrist</u>. <u>He</u> said he was fed up with people.

THE COMMA THAT DRESSES UP AS A FULL STOP

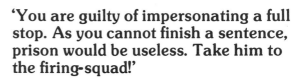

'You are guilty of impersonating a full stop. As you cannot finish a sentence, prison would be useless. Take him to the firing-squad!'

Write out the following, changing any 'dressed-up' commas into stops.

1 I am a clever farmer and I don't believe in wasting money, I have found an easy way to weigh a pig, there is no need to buy expensive scales, you take a long plank and place the plank across a stool, you get a big stone and put the pig on one end of the plank, put the stone on the other end and shift the position of the plank, make the pig and the stone balance each other, guess the weight of the stone and you have the weight of the pig.

2 John Smith desperately wanted to be a great actor, he went to an audition for the part of Abraham Lincoln, he dressed up to look exactly like the great man, wearing a top-hat, a red sash, black frock-coat and big shiny boots, he made his face up to look like Lincoln, with a big false nose and a fringe beard, he learnt by heart the famous speech Abraham Lincoln had made after the Battle of Gettysburg, but he did not get the part, he was assassinated on his way home.

3 A teacher asked her class to write an essay on Alfred the Great, she warned them not to drag in the old story of his burning the cakes, after she had read about half the essays and was congratulating herself on having got the message across, she picked up one which ended: 'King Alfred, while hunting, came upon a humble cottage, he knocked at the door and was invited in by a peasant woman, I am not allowed to say what happened after that.'

4 I learned to swim at a very early age, I was three years old when my parents once rowed me out to sea in a little boat until we were a mile from shore, they told me to swim back by myself, I quite liked the swim, it was the getting out of the sack that was difficult.

5 Generous terms offered for a cat lover, kindly home wanted for pedigree male Siamese cat, neutered, owner going abroad.

THE COMMA THAT MARKS OFF ITEMS IN A LIST

The hunter on safari has porters to carry the tinned food (comma), the whisky (comma), water for washing (comma), ammunition and sundries.

> **If a sentence contains a list of things, commas are used to mark off and separate each item.**

The last but one item in a list is usually joined with the word 'and' instead of a comma, but if the meaning is not absolutely clear, put a comma before the word 'and'.

If there should be a chance of confusion with another 'and', you must use a final comma. For example:

'When I win the pools, the woman in my life will wear furs and feathers, pearls and diamonds, (final comma) and satins and silks. My wife will be well-dressed, too.'

Write out the following, putting in all the commas for lists. All the other commas have been included.

1 A bride should have something old something new something borrowed something blue.

2 'Did you know I got 100% in the English exam? I got 40% in reading 30% in spelling and 30% in punctuation.'

3 Station announcer: 'The train now arriving at platforms four five six seven and eight is coming in sideways!'

4 Astrologer to client: 'If you had been born two days later, you would have been kind generous considerate and intelligent.'

5 'May I help you, Sir?'
'Yes, I want to buy a stick.'
'Yes, Sir. Shooting shaving walking lip or candle?'

6 'Tom Pearse, Tom Pearse, lend me your grey mare, all along, down along, out along, lee. For I want to go to Widdicombe Fair, with Bill Brewer Jan Stewer Peter Gurney Peter Davey Daniel Whiddon Harry Hawk and Old Uncle Tom Cobbleigh and all and Old Uncle Tom Cobbleigh and all.'

7 'Name five days of the week without saying "Monday Tuesday Wednesday Thursday or Friday".'
'The day before yesterday yesterday today tomorrow and the day after tomorrow.'

8 At the school camp, a contest was held for the oddest object found on the beach, and the result was – 1st Smith 2nd Jones 3rd Tims 4th Roberts and 5th Jenkins.

> **'You're keen on sport. How do you start a flea race?'**
> **'You say, "One, two, flea, go!"'**

THE COMMA THAT SETS APART NAMES AND TITLES

'I, Algernon Fitzgerald Bloggs, being of sound mind, do leave everything I own and possess to The Sunnyside Elephants' Home.'

> Commas are used to mark off a name, title, or a description inside a sentence.

Here is an example, in which the words marked off by commas are in italic so that they show up clearly.

Mrs Smith, *anxious mother of young Jimmy Smith*, to the Headmaster: '*Headmaster*, I want my son to stop learning French.'
'That, *Madam*, will present no difficulty whatsoever.'

Write out the following, putting in the commas to set apart names, etc. All the other commas needed, have been included.

1 'Mary to what family does the walrus belong?'
 'I don't know Miss. No family in our street has one.'
2 'Young man do you think you are doing the teaching in this class?'
 'No Sir you're the teacher.'
 'In that case boy stop acting like an idiot!'
3 'Some conjurors say that three is the magic number my dear boy and some say seven. It's neither my young friend Oliver neither. It's number one.'

4 'Dad Dr Brainstorm the head of the Department of Psychiatry at the hospital has diagnosed me as a kleptomaniac. Oh Dad whatever shall I do?'
 'Don't worry son of mine chip off the old block. The thing about kleptomania is, if you've got it, you can always take something for it.'
5 The botany lecturer a very experienced tutor gave his new young colleague fresh from university just one piece of advice: 'On field trips young fellow always walk well in front of your students, so that you can tramp on any specimens you don't recognize.'
6 A young lady whose name was Jones went to a newly opened branch of her bank to cash a cheque. She went to the counter of Miss Smith senior cashier and presented her cheque.
 'Good morning Madam,' said Miss Smith. 'Can you identify yourself?'
 The young lady Miss Jones opened her handbag, took out a mirror, looked into it, and said, 'Yes, it's me all right.'

> 'I say, Nurse, what would it take to make you give me a kiss?'
> 'You, Charlie? Chloroform!'

THE SLOW BUT SURE COMMA THAT MAKES YOUR MEANING CLEAR

> **Commas are used to tell the reader when to make a short pause. They divide a sentence into parts, making it easier to read and understand.**

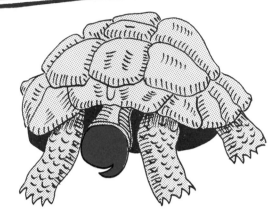

Use the comma only where you feel you need to make the reader pause in order to fully understand the sentence.

A A sentence with the comma purposely left out:
I am afraid I take the old-fashioned view the correct one.

Improved, with the comma put in:
I am afraid I take the old-fashioned view, the correct one.

B Two commas missing:
If she wins the beauty-contest she will be sent on holiday to Paris with her mother as a prize.

Without commas, this could read:
1 If she wins the beauty-contest
2 she will be sent on holiday to Paris
3 with her mother as a prize.

With the commas, the reader slows down long enough to divide the sentence correctly as:
If she wins the beauty-contest, she will be sent on holiday to Paris with her mother, as a prize.

C Here is a sentence, with one comma that should not be there:
If you buy your party drinks from us, we will supply you with free wine, and beer glasses.

Say why you think this is wrong, and write the sentence correctly.

D Write out the following, putting in the commas needed.

1 'Would you lend me £10 for a month old boy?'
2 'Let's go and watch the tigers eat Daddy.'
3 'You are so childish! Why don't you grow up stupid?'
4 If you can't make light of your troubles keep them dark.
5 If you want to keep a secret from your enemy do not tell your friend.
6 Those two are madly in love he with himself she with herself.
7 She picked up a bottle full of bitter rage and threw it at her husband's head.
8 He is a man aged forty-five whose wife has already left him and whose hair and teeth are seriously considering going too.
9 When you say that a person has a sense of humour do you mean that he makes you laugh or do you mean that you can make him laugh?

> **Work is the greatest thing in the world, (comma) so save plenty for tomorrow.**

THE SLOW BUT SURE COMMA THAT MAKES YOUR MEANING CLEAR

Write out the following, putting in all the commas needed.

1 A bore is a person who when you ask him how he is tells you.

2 The unexpected doesn't always happen but when it does it generally happens when you are least expecting it.

3 The most effective way to make people think something is not to talk about it but to take it for granted.

4 A statistician is a person who if you've got your feet in the oven and your head in the refrigerator will tell you that on average you are very comfortable.

5 Our planet goes on its course through space revolving towards the sun day and night night and day year in year out with a few thousand million people on board most of whom are not aware that the planet is moving.

6 We do some of our learning in school but we also learn from looking at the world around us talking to people reading books listening to the radio watching television playing games – everything teaches.

7 In war whichever side may call itself the victor there are no winners but all are losers.

8 Themistocles the great Athenian general on being asked whether he would choose to marry his daughter to a poor man of merit or to a worthless man of rich estate replied that he would prefer a man without an estate to an estate without a man.

9 The trouble with girls is if they like a boy no matter how arrogant he is they will say he has an inferiority complex and if they do not like a boy no matter how nice a person he is or how big an inferiority complex he has they will say that he is conceited.

10 Three men were on their way to rob a bank when they got stuck in the revolving doors. They had to be helped free by the staff and after thanking everyone sheepishly left the building.

A few minutes later they returned and announced their intention of robbing the bank but none of the staff believed them. When at first they demanded the sum of £50,000 the head cashier laughed at them convinced that it was a practical joke. Considerably disheartened by this the gang leader reduced his demand first to £5000 then to £500 and ultimately to £50. By this stage the cashier could barely control himself for laughter.

Then one of the men jumped over the counter and fell awkwardly on the floor clutching at his ankle. The other two made their getaway but got trapped in the revolving doors for a second time desperately pushing the wrong way.

Operating-theatre nurse:
'Shouldn't we do something about the bleeding, (comma) Doctor?

CAPITAL LETTERS

'Julius Caesar conquered North Africa; he conquered north of the Rhine; he conquered Gaul, and he conquered Britain.'
'Why did he stop?'
'He ran out of conkers!'

A   Unless they begin a sentence, ordinary words (common nouns) do not have a capital letter, but if they are used as part of a proper noun, a capital letter is needed.

Ordinary word	Proper noun
river	River Humber
bridge	Westminster Bridge
street	Downing Street
city	City of Birmingham
uncle	Uncle Ebenezer
lady	Lady Jane Grey

'Darling, you have the face of a saint,' said the girl, 'a Saint Bernard!'

B   In the caption to the picture, there is a word used on its own and also as part of a proper noun. What is the word?

> **There were two bishops in a bed.**
> **Which bishop wore the nightie?**
> **Mrs Bishop.**

C   Write out the following, changing small letters to capital letters where necessary.

1   sunday school teacher:
 'What happened on ascension day?'
 pupil: 'We had cream buns for tea.'

2   anthropologist: 'What did you red indians call america before the white man came?'
 red indian chief: 'Ours!'

3   'Did you watch "tomorrow's world" yesterday?'
 'No, I recorded it on my video; I shall see "tomorrow's world" tomorrow.'

4   An eight-year-old girl was taken to a coffee morning which, it was explained, was in aid of the save the children fund. 'Why?' she asked 'Are they becoming extinct?'

5   The great einstein once said, 'If my theory of relativity is proven successful, germany will claim me as a german and france will declare that I am a citizen of the world. Should my theory prove not true, france will say that I am a german, and germany will declare that I am a jew.'

6   A japanese lady went back to japan after having travelled a great deal on english trains. 'they are the best in the world,' she said, 'with special compartments for everybody. i have seen carriages not only labelled "smoking", but also "reading", "sandwich" and "bath"!'

> **A man was arrested today wearing only a newspaper. He said he liked to dress with *The Times*.**

CAPITAL LETTERS

'Why, hello, Mrs Robinson – I recognized you from Elizabeth's drawings.'

D When speaking of a person in a general way, use a small letter; when speaking of a particular person, use a capital letter, e.g.

(a) 'This is the <u>m</u>other of John.'
(b) 'Is tea ready yet, <u>M</u>other?'
(c) 'He is <u>h</u>eadmaster of a school.'
(d) 'The <u>H</u>eadmaster will see you.'

All the important words in the titles of books, plays, films, etc., have capital letters, e.g.:

A Tale of Two Cities (book)
The School for Scandal (play)
A Night at the Opera (film)

Note the following:
The letter 'I' is a capital when it stands on its own.

The words 'God' and 'He' (referring to God) must have capital letters.

Capitals are used for days of the week, months and holidays. Small letters are used for the seasons, and points of the compass:

<u>S</u>aturday, <u>F</u>ebruary, <u>E</u>aster
autumn,   south,   easterly

E Write out the following, changing small letters to capital letters, where necessary.

1 Club Notice: 'Our girl friday mans the phones between 9 a.m. and 12 noon on tuesdays and thursdays.

2 There's a new instant meal invented, based on duck. It's going to be called 'quick quack'.

3 teacher: 'elizabeth, give me a sentence beginning with "i".'
elizabeth: 'i is . . .'
teacher; 'elizabeth! you know you must always say "i am".'
elizabeth: 'All right, miss. i am the letter in the alphabet after h.'

4 The little girl said she had seen a lion in the rose garden, and for telling a lie, was sent to her room to apologize to god.
'Did you ask god to forgive you?' asked her mother, later.
'Yes, i did.'
'And what did he say?'
'Well, he said "That's funny, Elizabeth, because for a minute, i thought it was a lion, too."'

5 'Why is the isle of wight a fraud?'
'Because it has cowes you can't milk; freshwater you can't drink; newport you can't bottle, and needles you can't thread.'

6 During the war i worked for military intelligence. for my first assignment i was posted to the royal mint. i acted as a mint spy.

The following news item was printed wrongly. In your own words explain why it is wrong, and rewrite it correctly.

'England will win The Next World's Cup!'

There were three cats named Un, Deux and Trois. One day they went rowing, and what happened? Un, Deux, Trois cats sank!

THE DASH THAT INDICATES A SUDDEN CHANGE OF THOUGHT

I was an unwanted child — *my mother wanted puppies*

> **The dash is like a comma, but the pause is longer and the dash is stronger. It is used to mark a sudden turn in the thought of a sentence. It may also be used to mark an unexpected ending.**

A   The dash is used wrongly more often than any other punctuation mark.

1 Never use a dash when a comma is all that is needed.
2 Never use a dash in the place of a full stop.
3 Never use a dash unless it is absolutely necessary.

Example of a dash marking a break in thought:

When you are down and out, something always turns up – usually the noses of your friends.

B   Write out the following, putting in the dashes.

1 'Why don't you come to the pub with us, Charlie? Are you a man or a mouse?'
   'I'm a man my wife is scared of mice.'
2 Shop window sign: 'Try our easy terms 100% down and nothing more to pay.'

3 There are always two reasons for doing anything a good reason and the real reason.
4 I heard a voice inside me say, 'Smile! Things could be worse.' So I smiled and they got worse.
5 I have always believed in love at first sight ever since I looked into a mirror.
6 'No credit given except to people over 85, if accompanied by both parents.'
7 'Basset Hound for sale. May be seen at above address in the evening or heard within a mile radius at dawn.'
8 If you are in the jungle at night and you see two eyes staring at you, they may not be the eyes of a tiger they may be the eyes of two one-eyed tigers.
9 I like to be allowed to admire a person's opinion as I would his dog without being expected to take it home with me.
10 Adam was but human this explains it all. He did not want the apple for the apple's sake; he wanted it only because it was forbidden. The mistake was in not forbidding the serpent then he would have eaten the serpent.

> **'I've just lost my dog.'**
> **'Why don't you put an advert in the local paper?'**
> **'Don't be silly – my dog can't read.'**

THE DASH THAT LEADS TO THE UNEXPECTED

'I've come for the reward for returning your canary.'
  'That's not a canary. It's a cat!'
  'I know – the canary is in the cat.'

Example of a dash marking an unexpected ending:

'Say it with flowers – buy her a triffid.'

1 'Preserve wildlife pickle a squirrel!'
2 'My wife has a wonderful way of cutting a story short she interrupts.'
3 When our headmaster has you in his office, he becomes two people Mr Hyde and Mr Hyde.
4 The boss of my firm is an amazing fellow. He bites off more than he can chew and then chews it.
5 My brother was run over by a steam-roller. He's in hospital in rooms 22 to 29.
6 'They're a loving couple, aren't they?' 'Yes, he loves her for what she is rich.'
7 I'm off to the doctor's about my husband: I don't like the look of him.' 'I'll come with you I hate the sight of mine.'
8 'This is my last warning, you cad! If you don't stop fooling around with my wife I'm going to let you have her!'

D The dash may also be used:

1 to mark an afterthought:
   (a) 'You look like an accident – waiting to happen.'
   (b) 'I knew your father as a man, as an adolescent and as a child – sometimes on the same day.'
2 to separate a repetition:
   'Lord God of Hosts, be with us yet, Lest we forget – lest we forget.'
3 to mark an incomplete or interrupted sentence:
   'Why are you late?'
   'Sir, a sign down there – '
   'What has a sign to do with it?'
   'It said "School Ahead. Go Slow".'
4 to introduce or follow a list:
   (a) Walls may be hidden with climbing plants – ivy, honeysuckle, roses and clematis.
   (b) Weeping willows, silver birches, scarlet maples – all these trees grew in the splendid garden.

E Put dashes in the following:

The General met two soldiers carrying a large soup kettle from the kitchen. 'Here, you,' he barked, 'let me taste that!'
  'But, Gen'
  'Don't "but" me get a spoon!'
  The General tasted it and spat it out. 'You don't call that stuff soup, do you?' he roared.
  'No, sir,' replied the soldier. 'That's what I was trying to tell you it's dishwater!'

'My father may have a cold, hard exterior, but beneath it there beats a heart – a cold, hard heart.'

THE COMMA USED IN PARENTHESIS

Perfect happiness /even in memory/ is very rare.

PARENTHESIS

> A parenthesis is a word or a group of words put inside a sentence in order to give an explanation or a piece of extra information.

It is important to remember that no matter how long the statement in parenthesis may be, it is always an <u>addition</u> to the sentence. If the parenthesis is left out, the sentence must still make sense.

A parenthesis may be written in one of three different ways: (a) a pair of commas (b) a pair of dashes, and (c) a pair of brackets. How to choose among the three?

The pair of commas is used when the separated material is fairly close to the main meaning of the sentence.

Example, using comma parenthesis:

Operations, <u>like snooker championships</u>, make wonderful television.

Example, without the parenthesis:
Operations make wonderful television.

Write out the following, putting in the two commas for parenthesis. In addition underline the parenthesis. For example:

The hotel is within easy reach of Colchester, <u>the oldest town in Britain</u>, and many villages.

1 'What did the sergeant say when you called him a half-wit?'
'Well as a matter of fact I don't think he heard me.'

2 'Well, Son, did you pass your exam?'
'Not exactly to tell the truth but I was top of those who failed.'

3 There is nothing absolutely nothing a man cannot forget, except himself.

4 The Earth as everybody knows nowadays is a sphere slightly compressed orange fashion with a diameter of nearly 8,000 miles. Around the Earth circles a small sphere the Moon at an average distance of 239,000 miles.

5 The great secret known to doctors but still hidden from the general public is that most things get better by themselves.

6 People like peaches and pears grow sweet a little while before they begin to decay.

7 The law in its majestic equality forbids the rich as well as the poor to sleep under the arches.

8 I once went shopping for textbooks with my friend a petite blonde who had a long list. As we approached the counter balancing books in both hands the assistant said, 'It looks as though you're going to be the brightest girl in the class.'
'Well, I hope so,' she replied. 'I'm the teacher.'

THE DASH USED IN PARENTHESIS

'My promise – ask anybody – is my bond.'

Deciding whether to use commas or dashes for parenthesis is largely a matter of common sense. Commas are used much more frequently, but if the separated material is not very close to the main meaning, dashes should be used. For example:

Women – <u>one half the human race</u> – care more for a good marriage than for a great fortune.

Note that without the parenthesis, the sentence is still complete:

Women care more for a good marriage than for a great fortune.

Dashes are used for an interruption in the thought of a sentence, e.g.:

'I pledge you – <u>I pledge myself</u> – to a new deal for the American people.'

'She said – <u>I hope she is right</u> – that these samples are free.'

Dashes may be used to mark off a list:

Climbing plants – <u>clematis, honeysuckle, roses, ivy</u> – may be used to hide walls.

Dashes may be used for an 'afterthought':

Last Christmas – <u>I was with my family at the time</u> – I announced my engagement.

Write out the following, putting in the two dashes for parenthesis. In addition, underline the parenthesis.

1 Tom Smith is the goalkeeper probably the best in the country who has been picked to play for England next Saturday.

2 This restaurant chef has more than any other I know the art of making food look as good as it tastes.

3 The funniest news item I've read in a long time tells how *Animal Farm* George Orwell's satire on the totalitarian state got behind the Iron Curtain. It was included no one spotted it in the annual quota of farming books.

4 There are many reasons especially if one is a woman to be thankful for having been born in the twentieth century.

5 Francis Bacon believed rightly as we now know that science could provide a more powerful magic wand than the magicians had dreamed of.

6 If you wish to gain a reputation for being controversial in discussion, latch onto a topic on which there is universal agreement such as that eating people is wrong and say the opposite.

As the above will have shown, the difference between commas and dashes for parenthesis is mainly one of degree: the dashes are much stronger.

'Spare 50p, kind sir! All I own – apart from this gun – is £2.'

THE BRACKETS FOR THE 'ASIDE'

Animals that keep their young ones in pouches **marsupials** are to be found only in Australia.

> Brackets are used to enclose words which are not really part of the sentence but are added as an 'aside' to make the meaning more clear.

This is the third method of parenthesis and is much stronger than the other two (see page 14). The need to use brackets does not often occur, so care must be taken to limit their use. They should be reserved for cases where there is a definite intrusion into the thought process of the sentence; they should give the impression that the writer is passing on the words in brackets as though they were confidential.

Brackets do not need to have commas either in front or behind; they are, in fact, acting as very strong commas.

A Brackets are used to give additional information or explanation, e.g.:

1 Philately (<u>stamp</u> <u>collecting</u>) is an interesting and rewarding hobby.
2 Precious metals (<u>gold</u>, <u>silver</u> <u>and</u> <u>platinum</u>) are increasing in value.
3 All the survivors of the sunken vessel are well, including the captain's wife. She was insured (<u>the</u> <u>vessel</u>, <u>not</u> <u>the</u> <u>lady</u>) for a large sum and was heavily loaded with pig-iron.

B Note that if the parenthesis in brackets is omitted, the sentence is still complete. For example:

1 There is still time (<u>two</u> <u>months</u> <u>as</u> <u>the</u> <u>crow</u> <u>flies</u>) to organize an event for the local Bird-Watchers' Society.
2 There is still time to organize an event for the local Bird-Watchers' Society.

C Write out the following, putting in the two brackets for parenthesis. In addition, underline the parenthesis.

1 Winston Churchill Gt Britain and Charles de Gaulle France were the two greatest Europeans of the mid-twentieth century.
2 Mrs Smith used a little stone dog as a door stop for the nursery in case the baby cried at night. She thought it was as ugly as sin the dog, not the baby.
3 'Abou Ben Adhem may his tribe increase,
   Awoke one night from a deep dream of peace.'
4 If what the scientists claim is true and anything a scientist tells you should be taken with a pinch of sodium chloride I shall have to eat my words.
5 Woodwork Master holding up a piece of sandpaper: 'What is this I am holding?'
   Pupil a bit of a 'smart Alec': 'A map of the Sahara Desert, Sir.'

WORDS IN ITALICS AND WORDS UNDERLINED

> **Italics are used to call attention to a word or words as being distinct from the other words in the sentence.**

Italics (*letters which slant to the right like this*) are used in print, but in handwriting and typewriting, words which need to be given distinction are underlined instead.

The three main uses for italics are:

(a) to give special emphasis:
'Mum, I'm homesick.'
'But this *is* your home!'
'I know, and I'm sick of it!'

(b) to set out words in a foreign language (but not 'absorbed' words such as 'café', 'delicatessen', etc.):
The new opera received its world *première* last night, at Drury Lane.

(c) to set out the titles of published or performed works such as novels, newspapers, plays, films, *etc.* (as an alternative to quotation marks):
'Do you think the jokes in *Handling Punctuation* are as good as the ones in *Handling Spelling*?'

Avoid over-use of underlining for emphasis; if it becomes a habit for the usual, it is rendered useless for the unusual.

Write out the following, underlining words where necessary.

1 'What does coup de grâce mean?'
'It's French for lawn-mower.'

2 A drama critic once reviewed a play called Dreadful Night. His review read: 'Exactly.'

3 The only people who never believe in spiritualism are magicians and illusionists.

4 'Which is correct? Nine and five are thirteen, or nine and five is thirteen?'
'Neither: the answer is fourteen.'

5 St Mary's C. of E. School, Hendon, has as its motto, 'I hear, I see, I learn' – or, in Latin, Audio, Video, Disco.

6 Unlike vehicles using the flashing blue light, doctors driving cars using the flashing green light must observe the speed limits.

7 'I came top in the Comprehension test.'
'Did you, darling? You are a clever little boy.'
'Tell me, Mummy, just what is "comprehension"?'

8 Young men think old men are fools; old men know young men are fools.

9 At a smart restaurant, the maître d'hôtel was asked what he would do if a streaker turned up.
'First, Monsieur,' he said, 'I would give him a necktie. No one, but no one, is allowed in here without a tie.'

> **In the theatre one day, the stage manager asked where a certain actress was. 'She's round behind,' he was told, meaning backstage.**
> **'I know <u>that</u>,' he retorted, 'but <u>where is she?</u>'**

THE APOSTROPHE TO TELL WHO IS THE OWNER

THE BIRD (ITS)	SONG
THE BIRD ('S)	SONG
THE BIRD'S	SONG

THE BIRDS (THEIR)	SONGS
THE BIRDS ('')	SONGS
THE BIRDS'	SONGS

> **The apostrophe is used to show that something belongs to someone or something.**

(a) Where does the apostrophe go? Ask yourself 'Who is the owner?' and put the apostrophe after the last letter of the owner's name. If only one person owns something, use 's:
'Where is Hadrian's wall?'
'Please, Miss, on the side of Hadrian's house.'

(b) If more than one person owns something, add the apostrophe after the s:
'Mum, there's a man at the door collecting for the old folks' home.'
'Well, give him your grandfather.'

(c) If two or more named people own something, use 's after the last person only:
Mary and Jim's new car is a Rover.

(d) If the plural word of the owner does not end in s, use apostrophe s:
Women's guesses are much more accurate than men's certainties.

(e) If a person's name or profession already ends in s, use a second s only if you would sound it when speaking:

'Boss, the actress Jane Jenkins' leg was broken in a car accident!'
'OK. Take down this headline: "Actress's broken leg hits box office!"'

(f) You need an apostrophe for ownership even when there are no people or animals:

Monday's child is fair of face.
(Monday its child = Monday's child.)

The man who is everybody's friend is nobody's. i.e. nobody's friend.
(Nobody his friend = nobody's friend, because "nobody" has ownership.)

(g) You need an apostrophe s for the word 'one' when it shows ownership:
The worst evil of being in prison is that one can never lock one's door.

(h) Note the placing of the apostrophe in words ending in 'y' and 'ies':
Try to reduce an enemy's hatred, before it spreads to enemies' hatreds.

Write out the following, putting in all the apostrophes required.

1 A hen is only an eggs way of making other eggs.
2 The Puppeteers Union is asking for a pay increase with no strings attached.

3 On the menu of a snack bar: 'Todays special: ploughpersons lunch.'

4 Last weeks best headline: 'A farmers wife is best shot.'

5 'Why do demons and ghouls get along so well? Because demons are a ghouls best friend!'

6 A doctor and a boy were fishing. The boy was the doctors son, but the doctor was not the boys father. Who was the doctor? His mother.

7 The number of ducks killed on the road beside the duck-pond was being discussed. The Parish Councillors decision was that the fault lay with the ducks lack of road sense, not with the motorists.

8 News item: 'At the moment, the golf course is too short to attract the mens big tournaments, although we do get several large womens competitions.'

9 'A fools paradise is a wise mans hell,' he said, 'and a mans dying is more the survivors affair than his own.'

10 'A moments insight is sometimes worth a lifetimes experience,' she said, 'and to ease anothers heartache, is to forget ones own.'

11 During our drama groups regular visits to an open prison, the prisoners heckling was a challenge to the actors self-control. On one occasion it was completely shattered.

'But, Mum,' ran the line, 'I am innocent!'

Back came a chorus of two hundred voices: 'So was I, mate!'

12 A man went for a brain transplant and was offered the choice of two brains – an architects for £1,000 and a politicians for £10,000.

'Does that mean the politicians brain is ten times better than the architects?' asked the man.

'No,' was the reply, 'the politicians has never been used.'

KING CHARLES (HIS)   HEAD
KING CHARLES   ('S)   HEAD
KING CHARLES'S   HEAD

13 'I hear you had a gentlemens agreement with your late partner. Did he leave you his share of the business profits?'

'No. He turned it all into travellers cheques, and took it with him.'

14 '. . . And the wheels kick,
And the winds song and the white
sails shaking,
And a grey mist on the seas face, and
a grey dawn breaking.
I must go down to the seas again,
to the vagrant gypsy life,
To the gulls way and the whales way,
where the winds like a whetted knife.'

15 Tongue-twister: 'The sixth sick sheikhs sixth sheeps sick.'

16 Because of the two companies merger, each companys employees have had to be issued with a new employers contract.

17 An ounce of a persons own wit is worth a ton of other peoples.

'What is Father Christmas's wife's name?'
'Mary Christmas!'

THE APOSTROPHE TO REPLACE LETTERS LEFT OUT

> The apostrophe is used to show that a letter or letters have been missed out.

The apostrophe to replace letters left out is used mainly in writing down conversation; it helps to make the words flow more rapidly.

(a) It is usually used to shorten two words into one word, for example:

1 'Where is the dog, Charlie?'
'I am afraid I have had him put away.'
'Was he mad?'
'He was not exactly pleased.'
2 'Where's the dog, Charlie?'
'I'm afraid I've had him put away.'
'Was he mad?'
'He wasn't exactly pleased.'

(b) It is used to show that a letter has been left out owing to incorrect pronunciation.

'I call my dog Isaiah.'
'Why's that?'
'Because one eye's 'igher than the other.'

(c) The apostrophe for 'would' is 'd.

'If I had either of you two as my wife I'd poison your tea.'
'If we had you as a husband, we'd drink it!'

(d) This is a special occasion for using the apostrophe:

Teacher, to boy arriving late:
'You should have been here at nine o'clock!'
'Why, what happened?'

Note: Make sure that the apostrophe goes in the space where the missing letter or letters should be.

A Write out the following, putting in all the missing apostrophes.

1 'Doctor, I need something for my kidneys!'
'OK. Heres some bacon.'
2 'Why do you have a carrot sticking out of your ear?'
'I cant hear you. Ive got a carrot sticking out of my ear.'
3 I know Im not much, but Im all Ive got.
4 You cant expect a boy to be vicious till hes been to a good school.
5 'I met Patrick OBrien today, and I hadnt seen him for ten years.'
'Tell me, has he kept his youthful figure?'
'Kept it? Hes doubled it!'

'A smile 🐬s the way...'

**A SMILE IS THE WAY TO START THE DAY.
A SMILE'S THE WAY TO START THE DAY.**

6 First cannibal: 'I dont think much of your husband.'
Second cannibal: 'Thats all right. Eat the vegetables instead.'

7 Sergeant to his platoon in church: 'Ats off, you lot! We are in the ouse o God. Line up in fours!'

8 In the window of a venetian-blind shop: 'If it werent for us, itd be curtains for everybody!'

9 'Our caretakers eighty years old and hes still not got a grey hair on his head.'
'Whys that?'
'Hes bald!'

10 Nervous lady to pilot: 'Youll bring me down safely, wont you?'
'Dont worry, lady. Ive never left anybody up there yet.'

11 'Why are you searching the beach?'
'For a piece of toffee,' said hubby.
'Dont lets waste time doing that.'
'Well have to,' he said, 'my false teeth are stuck to it.'

B   Write out the following, using an apostrophe to shorten the two words underlined, into one word.

1 If it <u>were</u> <u>not</u> for the optimist, the pessimist <u>would</u> <u>not</u> know how happy he <u>was</u> <u>not</u>.

2 Wife to husband: 'I <u>did</u> <u>not</u> say there <u>were</u> <u>not</u> two sides to every story – I just said I <u>was</u> <u>not</u> listening to your side.'

3 'If <u>you</u> <u>will</u> give me your phone number, young lady, <u>I</u> <u>will</u> call you up some time.'
'<u>It</u> <u>is</u> in the book.'
'Fine! And <u>what</u> <u>is</u> your name?'
'<u>That</u> <u>is</u> in the book, too.'

4 'Men, fire at will!'
'Sir,' a soldier shouted, '<u>we</u> <u>have</u> been firing for an hour and run out of ammunition!'
'We <u>must</u> <u>not</u> let the enemy know that,' roared the officer. 'Keep firing!'

5 In an optician's shop window: 'If you <u>do</u> <u>not</u> see what you want, <u>you</u> <u>have</u> come to the right place.'

6 A man was examining the household accounts kept by his wife.
'Well, my dear,' he said, '<u>you</u> <u>will</u> be interested to know that <u>we</u> <u>have</u> now come to the bridge which we said <u>we</u> <u>would</u> cross when we came to it.'

7 Dear Miss Smith,
   <u>I</u> <u>have</u> not sent Johnny to school this morning because he <u>has</u> <u>not</u> been. <u>I</u> <u>have</u> given him something to make him go, and when <u>he</u> <u>has</u> been <u>he</u> <u>will</u> come.

8 When I answered the phone, a male voice said, 'Come on over.' I <u>did</u> <u>not</u> reply.
'Come on, <u>we</u> <u>are</u> waiting,' the voice said, rather impatiently.
'To whom do you wish to speak?' I said. There was a long pause, and then the answer, '<u>I</u> <u>am</u> sorry, lady, <u>I</u> <u>have</u> got the wrong number. Nobody I know says "whom".'

'What's the matter, son?' asked the store detective.
'I've lost my mum,' said the child.
'What's your mum like?'
'Guinness and bingo.'

THE APOSTROPHE TO SHORTEN WORDS USED IN SPEECH

There are some pairs of words which are almost always used as a single word with an apostrophe, when used in speech. For example: you are = you're, we are = we're, they are = they're.

'**Your** altimeter is faulty! **You're** coming in too low, **you're** coming in too . . .'

You must never use an apostrophe unless a letter or letters have been left out. When in doubt, read the sentence to find out if the word is single, or made up of two words.

'<u>Your</u> altimeter is faulty!'
This is one word, so no apostrophe is required. (You could not say '<u>You</u> <u>are</u> altimeter is faulty!')
'<u>You're</u> coming in too low!'
   This is really '<u>You</u> <u>are</u> coming in too low!' The two words 'you are' are shortened by leaving out the 'a' and replacing it with an apostrophe.

Similar pairs of words are:

we are – becomes – we're
they are – becomes – they're

If we realize that we aren't as wise today as we thought we <u>were</u> yesterday, <u>we're</u> wiser today.

A visitor to a country church remarked that <u>there</u> (not 'they are') was a lot of coughing during the sermon.
'<u>They're</u> not coughs,' he was told, '<u>they're</u> time signals.'

Write out the following, putting in all the apostrophes needed.

1 'Whats 4Q plus 6Q?'
   'Ten Q.'
   'Youre welcome!'
2 Why do leopards never escape from zoos? Because theyre always spotted.
3 'I don't care if youre Santa Claus, get your reindeer off my roof!'
4 Lets be happy while were living, for were a long time dead.
5 Teenage girl to father behind newspaper: 'I know that youre listening, Dad – your knuckles are white!'
6 'You couldn't fly your rocket-ship to the sun, youd be burnt to a crisp!'
   'That's where youre wrong, clever; Id land at night!'
7 They keep saying theyre not afraid to die. Well, neither am I; I just dont want to be there when it happens.
8 Shop window notice: 'Were the best store in town, and were open all day Saturday.'
9 'Im sorry, but youve got the wrong number. Theres no Fred here.'
   'Dont be sorry, lady. Youre lucky you dont know him.'

'Why is your dog glaring at me like that?'
'Take no notice. It's just that you're eating from its dish.'

'You're eating from <u>its</u> dish.'
This is one word, so no apostrophe is needed. (You could not say 'You're eating from <u>it is</u> dish.')

'<u>It's</u> just that you're eating . . .'
This is really '<u>It is</u> just that . . .'
The two words 'it is' are shortened by leaving out the 'i' and putting an apostrophe in its place.

Similar pairs of words are:
who is – becomes – who's

The pig <u>whose</u> (not '<u>who is</u>') house was built of bricks, sang: '<u>Who's</u> ('who is') afraid of the big bad wolf?'

let us – becomes – let's

The window <u>lets</u> (not 'let us') in a draught; <u>let's</u> ('let us') open the door instead.

there is (and there has) – there's
that is (and that has) – that's
he is (and he has) – he's
it is (and it has) – it's

'Stop, Henry! <u>That's</u> not our baby!'
'<u>It's</u> not? Oh, well, <u>there's</u> no sense in fussing. <u>Let's</u> take it: <u>it's</u> a better pram.'

A Write out the following, putting in the apostrophes.

1 'I want you to keep that dog out of my house – its full of fleas!'
'Come along, Pongo. Were not going into a house thats full of fleas.'
2 'I've been feeding my dog plenty of garlic.'
'What on earth for?'
'To make sure that its bark is worse than its bite.'
3 'Thats a lovely bulldog you have there, with its fine, dignified flat face.'
'Its not a bulldog. It was chasing a cat, and ran into a wall.'
4 'Its not my fault!' declared the truculent camel, refusing to break its back with someone elses last straw.
5 'Knock, knock!'
'Whos there?'
'Irish stew.'
'Irish stew who?'
'Irish stew in the name of the law.'

B Write out the following, putting either <u>his</u> or <u>he's</u> in the spaces.

1 A man and ____ wife had gone away on holiday, leaving their dog in a dog's home. When they returned, the husband collected ____ dog and drove home with it.
'I don't know what's the matter with him,' he said. '____ been barking all the way home. Do you think ____ homesick for the kennels?'
'No,' said ____ wife, 'What ____ been trying to tell you is that ____ the wrong dog.'

'Knock, knock.'
'Who's there?'
'You're a lady.'
'You're a lady who?'
'I didn't know you could yodel.'

THE HYPHEN THAT JOINS WORDS TOGETHER

> When two or more words are considered to be a single expression, we connect these words with hyphens.

Note: A hyphen is half the length of a dash, and there is no space between a hyphen and the word it joins. For example:

After an accident between a <u>cement-mixer</u> and a <u>prison-van</u>, police are looking for six hard men.

A   Write out the following, putting in all the hyphens required.

1 'Why is your brother so small?'
   'Because he's my half brother.'
2 Seen in the back window of a very old car: 'My other car is a Rolls Royce.'
3 'Waiter, I'd like to know where you get such large mussels.'
   'I do weight lifting, sir.'
4 'I hear you've been in hospital.'
   'I only went in for a brain scan, but they said they found nothing.'
5 News item: 'Today, the East German pole vault champion became the West German pole vault champion.'
6 'I don't know how it can tell, but a thermos flask keeps hot things hot and cold things cold.'
7 'Where's the sun lounge?'
   'Outside the betting shop with his father.'
8 What do you call a frog spy? A croak and dagger agent.
9 One mouse fell off the wall; what did the other mouse do? He used mouse to mouse resuscitation.

10 'With what do you connect the name Baden Powell?'
   'A hyphen.'

B   The hyphen is used in writing fractions and compound numbers, e.g.

1 One-third of the people in this village don't know how the other three-quarters lives.
2 When my Dad was twenty-one, he was a seven-stone weakling; he's forty-two now, and he's a fourteen-stone weakling.

C   Sometimes, a hyphen is used to join a prefix to a word, for example:

ex-captain   anti-climax   pre-war
co-operate   re-enter   semi-detached

D   Sometimes, the use of a hyphen is important to avoid giving the reader a wrong meaning. Compare the following:

1 I have a grand daughter of twelve.
   I have a grand-daughter of twelve.

2 She caught the ball on the rebound.
   This book will have to be re-bound.

3 The class contains ten year-old boys.
   The class contains ten-year-old boys.

'Your Honour, I began life as a poor bare-footed child.'

'That's no excuse: nobody is born with shoes.

An important use of the hyphen is making a compound adjective from two connected words, for example:

'You know my water-proof, rust-resistant, anti-magnetic, shock-absorbing pocket-watch? Well, it just caught fire!'

E Write out the following, putting in all the hyphens required.

1 In the country of the blind, the one eyed man is king.
2 'Visit our stores for quick and courteous self service.'
3 For sale: small red faced lady's wrist watch.
4 When your friends tell you how young you look, you're middle aged.
5 'What's your son going to be when he's passed his exams?'
'An old age pensioner!'
6 'Give me an example of wasted energy.'
'Telling a hair raising story to a bald headed man.'

7 Headline: 'One legged man denies kicking platform ticket machine.'
8 'What do you have if you cross a monster with a drip dry suit?
A wash and 'were' wolf!

F The hyphen is used when splitting a word <u>between</u> <u>syllables</u> at the end of a line. When doing so, make certain that each of the two parts can be properly pronounced, e.g.

tele- phone (<u>not</u> telep-hone)
happi- ness (<u>not</u> hap-piness)
screw- driver (<u>not</u> screwd-river)

G The hyphen may be used to group together a set of words that you would like to be read as one unit, for example:

Gibbs designed St Martin-in-the-Fields.
The film shows some incredible-but-true revelations about the Kaiser.

H Write out the following, putting in all the hyphens needed.

1 I don't want to be a might have been!
2 If my husband ever had any get up and go, it got up and went before I met him.
3 The detective thought that the case of the missing umbrellas was a put up job and strictly for the undercover agents' fair weather boys.

I The hyphen may be used to separate letters for a special purpose, e.g.:

'I've lost my hearing-aid; please speak to me v-e-r-y s-l-o-w-l-y.'

'Captain Kirk, the rocket-motor's just fallen off! It could spell disaster!'
'What did you say, Scotty?'
'Spell disaster, Captain!'
'D-I-S-A-S-T-E-R.'

THE FULL STOP FOR ABBREVIATIONS

ABBREVIATION (noun)
= something shortened

> An abbreviation is a shortened word (or a group of words) usually marked with a full stop.

Most abbreviations require the use of a full stop but the following are exceptions:

  (a) metric measurements:
    mm mg cm cg km kg
  (b) shortened words widely accepted into common use:
    phone advert gym vet flu
  (c) words which end with the last letter of the complete word:
    Mr (<u>M</u>iste<u>r</u>) Mrs (<u>M</u>istres<u>s</u>)
    St (<u>St</u>ree<u>t</u>) Ltd (<u>L</u>imite<u>d</u>)
  (d) 'acronyms' (words made out of the initials of a group of words):
    ERNIE (<u>E</u>lectronic <u>R</u>andom <u>N</u>umber <u>I</u>ndicating <u>E</u>quipment)
    UNESCO (<u>U</u>nited <u>N</u>ations <u>E</u>ducational, <u>S</u>cientific, and <u>C</u>ultural <u>O</u>rganization)
  (e) initials of a group of words for which the full stop is not now used because of popular acceptance:
    VAT (<u>v</u>alue <u>a</u>dded <u>t</u>ax)
    BBC (<u>B</u>ritish <u>B</u>roadcasting <u>C</u>orp.)
    ITV (<u>I</u>ndependent <u>T</u>ele<u>v</u>ision)
    POW (<u>p</u>risoner <u>o</u>f <u>w</u>ar)

O   **QUESTION:**
B.A. **What does this say?**
M.A. **ANSWER:**
Ph.D. **Three degrees below zero!**

Match the abbreviations in the first list with the complete words set out in the second list, e.g.: dept.   department

dept.	N.S.P.C.C.	B.A.
asst.	P.T.O.	Y.W.C.A.
Ph.D.	anon.	O.H.M.S.
e.g.	R.A.F.	Jan.
i.e.	P.D.S.A.	W.H.O.
etc.	Nov.	capt.
Thurs.	R.S.P.C.A.	abbr.
Tues.	R.S.V.P.	Rev.
B.Sc.	M.O.T.	Hants.
A.D.	Exod.	q.e.d.
V.C.	Chas.	C.I.D.

Tuesday, World Health Organization, please turn over, Bachelor of Arts, Charles, <u>quod erat demonstrandum</u>, department, Victoria Cross, <u>id est</u>, On Her Majesty's Service, captain, Hampshire, Reverend, January, <u>répondez s'il vous plaît</u>, National Society for the Prevention of Cruelty to Children, assistant, Ministry of Transport, Exodus, Royal Air Force, Young Women's Christian Association, anonymous, Bachelor of Science, abbreviation, <u>Anno Domini</u>, Doctor of Philosophy, Peoples' Dispensary for Sick Animals, <u>et cetera</u>, Thursday, November, Criminal Investigation Department, Royal Society for the Prevention of Cruelty to Animals, <u>exempli gratia.</u>

> A little girl opened an invitation addressed to her father.
>   'What's that in aid of?' he asked.
>   'I think it's some kind of animal charity,' she replied. 'It's from the R.S.V.P.'

THE EXCLAMATION MARK

Exclamation mark used for a command

Exclamation mark used for an appeal

> **The exclamation mark is used to give a special, stronger meaning that a full stop cannot give. When it completes a sentence (in the same way as a full stop) the next word begins with a capital letter.**

Do not use the exclamation mark unless it is really needed. It should be used only for the following:

   (a) to give a command:
   The travelling salesman said that he had received three orders that day: 'Get out! Stay out! Don't come back!'
   (b) to express an appeal:
   'Spare a fiver, kind sir! All I have in the world is this revolver.'
   (c) for astonishment, surprise, or
       bewilderment:
   I heard a voice inside me say, 'You should smile; things could be worse.' So I smiled, and they got worse!
   (d) to display anger, or to make a loud
       exclamation:
   'Boy, I don't want you acting the fool in my class!'
   'But, Sir, I'm not acting!'

Note: In comics, cartoons and in advertisements, you sometimes see exclamation marks in groups of two or three. This is quite wrong.

Write out the following, putting in the required exclamation marks and any other punctuation needed.

1 Did you hear about the ship that sailed from Hong Kong with a cargo of yo-yos? It sank seventeen times

2 My brother's so tough, he could kick-start Concorde

3 Be a missionary Give cannibals a taste of christianity

4 At bedtime a mother opened the book her five year old had selected all on his own from the library
'Jack,' she exclaimed. 'This book is written in french'
'What a relief,' said the boy, 'I thought I had forgotten how to read'

5 After my first day at school i went home in a smouldering temper
'They never gave me the present'
'Present what present'
'They said they would give me a present'
'Well now im sure they didnt'
'They did they said youre jane smith arent you well just you sit there for the present i sat there all day but i never got it i aint going back there again'

> 'Waiter! What's the chicken like?'
> 'It doesn't like anything, sir. It's dead!'

QUOTATION MARKS USED FOR CONVERSATION

> **Quotation marks are used to show that somebody has spoken.**

Quotation marks (which are also known as 'speech marks' and 'inverted commas') are always used in pairs. They may be written as singles ('____') or as doubles ("____"). When printed (as in this book) they are in singles, but in writing, it is usual to use double quotation marks.

Only the words <u>actually</u> <u>spoken</u> go inside the quotation marks; all other words are outside, for example:

'You have a blank expression on your face, Johnny,' said the teacher. 'Do you have trouble hearing me?'

'No, Miss,' he replied, 'I have trouble listening.'

There are four ways in which spoken words may be set out, as follows:

(a) spoken words only:
'In this book, you will find much useful information.'

(b) <u>unspoken</u> words to introduce the spoken words:
The author said, 'In this book, you will find much useful information.'

   Note that <u>In</u> has a capital letter even though it follows a comma, because a capital is always used whenever a person begins to speak.

(c) <u>unspoken</u> words following the spoken words:
'In this book, you will find much useful information,' said the author.

Note that <u>said</u> does not have a capital letter, because although it is an unspoken word, it is part of the sentence.

(d) spoken words interrupted by <u>unspoken</u> words:
'In this book,' said the author, 'you will find much useful information.'

   Note that there is a comma after <u>book</u>, to separate it from the unspoken words, and a comma after <u>author</u> to separate the <u>unspoken</u> words from the spoken words which are following.

   Note also that <u>you</u> does not have a capital letter as it is part of the sentence, and that the full stop at the end is <u>inside</u> the quotation mark.

It is important to observe that as each person takes a turn to speak, a new line must be used, for example:

A small girl, absent from school for two days, returned on the third day.

'Hallo, Katie,' said her teacher. 'Why have you been away from school?'

'Sorry, Miss, but my dad got burnt.'

'Oh, dear!' said the teacher. 'Nothing serious, I hope.'

'They don't mess about at the crematorium, Miss.'

'Perkins, don't you know the bell has gone?'
'No, Sir, but I'm not surprised. They'll pinch anything in this school.'

A Write out the following, putting in all the quotation marks needed for spoken words.

1 If you had ten potatoes and had to divide them equally between seven persons, how would you do it?
I would mash the potatoes.

2 Does the Sergeant know about this? asked the Colonel, looking at a collapsed wall of sandbags.
He ought to, Sir, he's underneath.

3 Two men were sitting in a crowded bus. One of them had his eyes closed. What's the matter, Bill? the other asked, Feeling ill?
I'm all right, Sam, but I can't bear to see ladies standing.

4 The phone in the maternity ward rang and an excited voice said: I'm bringing my wife – she's going to have a baby!
Is this her first baby? asked the nurse.
No, came the reply, this is her husband.

5 A man found that one of the players at the poker-table was a dog, and remarked to his host, What a wonderful dog. He must be highly intelligent to be able to play poker.
Yes, but he plays badly, said the host. Whenever he gets a good hand, he wags his tail.

6 Circus lion to new lion just joining the team: You would have loved our last trainer; he looked after us with kindness and dedication.
New lion: Why did he leave?
He didn't. We ate him!

B Write out the following, putting in all the quotation marks, and starting a new line where required.

1 A friend once arranged a blind date for me. I waited patiently under the clock, as arranged, and eventually a pretty girl walked by. I said, Are you Evelyn? She said, Are you Reginald? I said, Yes. She said, I'm not Evelyn.

2 A woman with a baby in her arms was sitting in a railway station waiting-room, crying. A porter came up to her and asked what the trouble was. Some people were in here just now and they were so rude about my son, she cried. They all said he was ugly. There, there, don't cry, said the porter kindly. Shall I get you a nice cup of tea? Oh, that would be nice, said the woman, wiping her eyes. You are very kind. That's all right, said the porter, and while I'm at it, I'll get a banana for your monkey.

THE QUESTION MARK

> **The question mark is placed at the end of a question. When it completes a sentence (in the same way as a full stop) the next word begins with a capital letter.**

The question mark stands at the end of a <u>direct</u> question (never after an <u>indirect</u> question). For example:

(a) 'What do you call a budgie run over by a lawn-mower?' (direct question)

She asked me what I would call a budgie run over by a lawn-mower. (indirect question – no question mark)

What's the answer? Shredded tweet.

(b) 'I wondered how long a person could live without brains (indirect question – no question mark) so I am asking you. Tell me, how long can a person live without brains?' (direct question)
'How old are you?' you said.

Do not use a question mark when it is obvious that an answer is not really needed or expected. Example:
(a)'He's not exactly a master of tact, is he!' (exclamation mark or full stop instead)
When using quotation marks, remember that the question mark is followed by the

final quotation mark. 'Do you understand me<u>?</u>'

Write out the following, putting in the question marks needed, and any other punctuation marks.

1 Who is wise He who learns from all men.
2 'Dr Livingstone, I presume'
3 Doctor, I keep thinking I'm invisible Who said that
4 Waiter to diner: Do we honour credit cards Sir, we venerate them
5 What makes you think that Rome was built during the night
  Rome wasn't built in a day, was it
6 What's that you're making, James
  It's a portable, Sir.
  A portable what
  I don't know yet, Sir, I've only made the handles.
7 Did the stone fall on the clay pot
  Woe to the clay pot
  Did the clay pot fall on the stone
  Woe to the clay pot
8 Sir do you know that the most intelligent person in the world has gone deaf
      Is this another of your silly jokes boy
  Pardon
9 Want to buy a watch
  Who me yes how much
      Sh . . . sh . . . The fellow next to you is still wearing it
10 She offered me this dud £5 note your honour
  Counterfeit
  Yes your honour she had two

> **'Doctor, I've lost my memory!'**
> **'When did this happen?'**
> **'When did what happen?'**

Write out the following, putting in all the question marks, adding any other punctuation marks needed, and starting a new line where necessary, for each speaker.

1 'Can you help me out'
'Yes, which way did you come in'

2 'And when did your son first feel what it was like to be wanted' 'When he saw his name on a poster outside the police station'

3 Two men were out hunting. 'Hey, Bill.' 'What do you want' 'Are you all right' 'Yeah!' 'That's all right then; I've shot a bear.'

4 'I hear your husband is in hospital whats wrong with him' 'Hes suffering from fallen arches' 'Bad feet' 'No, a railway bridge fell on him'

5 Who was your mother Never had none said the child Never had any mother what do you mean where were you born Never was born persisted Topsy

6 Darling marvellous news Soon therell be three of us Really when Tomorrow Youre to pick up my mother at the station at four o'clock

7 How did you get on in the maths exam I only got one sum wrong thats very good how many were there ten does that mean you had nine right no they were the ones I couldnt do

8 May I have two weeks off work
What for
I'm getting married
But you've only just come back from three weeks in Devon why didn't you get married then
What and ruin my summer holiday

9 Alfred Hitchcock's occupation was listed as 'Producer' on his passport On one occasion a customs official asked producer what do you produce with a smile Hitchcock replied gooseflesh

10 If you prick us do we not bleed if you tickle us do we not laugh if you poison us do we not die and if you wrong us shall we not revenge

11 The following letter was sent to a newspaper editor from a reader on page five of last fridays issue there is the headline: "Whom should be laid off first" the answer is obvious whom wrote the headline him should be laid off first him doesnt know enough about grammar for the position him has does him

12 What! No star and you are going out to sea marching and you have no music travelling and you have no book what no love and you are going out to live

'This £10,' said the Fortune-teller, entitles you to ask two questions.'
'Isn't that a great deal of money for just two questions?'
  'Yes. What is your second question?'

'Tell me, why do you always answer a question with a question?'
'Why not?'

THE THREE DOTS

A row of three dots (an 'ellipsis') may be used in four different ways, to show that some letters or some words have been purposely left out.

'Charge! The enemy couldn't hit an elephant at this dist . . .'

1 In dialogue to indicate an interruption, for example:

> Angler: 'Talking about fishing, reminds me of the time . . .'
> Bored listener: 'Good Lord, you're right. I had no idea it was so late.'

2 To show that some quoted material has been left out:

> 'Anything you say . . . in evidence.'

or that only a small part is given:

> To be, or not to be, that is the question . . .'

3 To provide a pause:

> 'Who will change old lamps for new? . . . New lamps for old?'

or for a pause with a special effect:

> The Third World War had come to an end, and as the sun set slowly in the east . . .

4 To introduce a surprise:

> Think of a number between one and fifty. Double it, subtract four, add thirty, subtract the number you started with, close your eyes . . . dark, isn't it?

Write out the following, putting in the three dots where required.

1 Science has promised us truth it has never promised us happiness.
2 Don't drink and drive one swallow can make a summons.
3 'Somebody's boring me I think it's me.'
4 Sign outside a church: 'What is missing from this CHCH? UR!'
5 When he was learning to count, a small boy kept missing out the number six and had to be corrected each time. One day he was heard quietly rehearsing: 'One two three four five seven what-about-six eight nine.'
6 'I hear you buried your husband last week.'
'Had to dead you know. He died of a sore throat.'
'Nonsense! No one dies of a sore throat!'
'He did I cut it.'
7 'I used to be a were-wolf, but I'm much better now-oo-ow-ooo'

'If I had finished this sentence . . .'

QUOTATION MARKS USED TO PICK OUT SPECIAL WORDS

> Quotation marks may be used to call attention to a word or words as being distinct from the others in the sentence.

A Apart from the use of quotation marks to indicate words that are spoken, the four main uses for quotation marks are:

(a) to write the titles of books, plays, films, television programmes, newspapers, songs, poems, etc., e.g. There is a review of the opera 'Madam Butterfly' in 'The Times'.

(b) to quote from a published work: The first line of Shakespeare's 'Twelfth Night' is: 'If music be the food of love, play on . . .'

(c) to point out foreign words, slang, or specialist words, e.g.

1 The prices on this menu for 'À la carte' are lower than those for the 'Table d'hôte'.
2 Try as they might, the 'fuzz' just could not get the suspect to 'grass'.
3 She is a good 'A'-level candidate.
4 A cassette recorder handles the 'software' (the technical term for the various computer programmes).

(d) to show that words are being used in a humorous or a sarcastic manner, e.g.

1 My hotel doorman calls himself a 'taxidermist', because he stuffs people into cabs.
2 To say that Columbus 'discovered' America is sheer arrogance: millions of people were living there before 1492.
3 It is spring, and the travel agents are busily peddling their 'wheres'.

The quotation marks make me strong enough to stand as a 'special' word.

B Write out the following, putting in all the quotation marks needed.

1 Of all the words of tongue and pen, the saddest are, It might have been.
2 The cable address of the Yard's Murder Squad is Handcuffs, London.
3 A London Transport poster showed King Henry VIII asking for Tower Hill return. Underneath, someone had added: And a single for the wife.
4 In last week's Express and Independent, our parliamentary candidate wrote to say that she hoped to meet any of her constituents in prison. It should, of course, have read in person.
5 A Russian had to complete a questionnaire. To place of birth he answered: St Petersburg; as to education, he stated he was educated in Petrograd; his response as to where he lived now, was Leningrad. To the question Where would you like to live? he replied: St Petersburg.

QUOTATION MARKS INSIDE QUOTATION MARKS

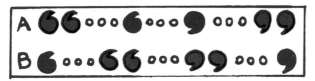

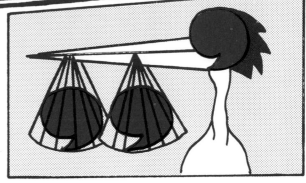

> Quotation marks inside quotation marks are used when you need to quote the <u>actual</u> words spoken.

As the above drawing shows, if you are using double quotation marks, the <u>inside</u> quotation marks must be single. This is in order to avoid confusing one set with the other. If, however, you are using single quotation marks, the <u>inside</u> marks must be double. The following illustrates both styles:

'What goes "oom oom" and "moo moo"?'
'A cow walking backwards and forwards.'

"What goes 'oom oom' and 'moo moo'?"
"A cow walking backwards and forwards."

Note that the question mark and the full stop are placed <u>inside</u> the final quotation mark.

Quotation marks inside quotation marks are also used to draw attention to a word or a group of words that have not been actually spoken, for example:

'What is the meaning of "fear"?'
'I don't know – I'm too afraid to ask.'

A   Write out the following, putting in the quotation marks inside quotation marks to quote the actual words spoken.

1   'Did you hear about the owl who went tweet, tweet? He didn't give a hoot.'

2   Farmer (to new hired hand): 'Where's that mule I told you to take out and have shod?'
New Hand: 'Did you say shod? I thought you said shot. I've just buried it.'

3   'To what do you owe your great success as a door-to-door salesman?'
'To the first words I say when a woman opens the door – Miss, is your mother in?'

4   'My dad used to be a lion-tamer. He ended his act by sticking his right hand into the lion's mouth. They used to call him Fearless.'
'What do they call him now?'
'Lefty.'

B   Do the same for the following, to draw attention to certain words.

1   'Johnny, give me a sentence containing the word officiate.'
'Please, Miss, I know a man who got sick from a fish he ate.'

2   'Was the new baby a nice pink and white colour?'
'No, it was a horrible yeller.'

3   'Don't be afraid of Rover, little boy. You know the saying, A barking dog never bites, don't you?'
'I know it and you know it,' said the boy, 'but does the dog know it?'

Write out the following, putting in
(a) the quotation marks and (b) the
quotation marks inside quotation marks.
Remember to start a new line whenever
there is a change of speaker.

1 Did you hear about the two
   blood-cells? They loved in vein.
2 Bull (singing a love-song): When I fall
   in love, it will be for heifer.
3 Student: Please engrave on this ring
   the words From Charles to Susan.
   Jeweller: Take my advice, young man,
   and shorten it to From Charles.
4 What is meant when a hill is described
   as 1 in 10, Mary? Please, Miss, it
   means there are nine others like it.
5 Pompous employer: I don't like yes
   men. When I say No, I want them to
   say No too.
6 Are you going to my party, Sally? No,
   I ain't going. Now you know what our
   teacher told us. Not aint. It's, I am not
   going, he is not going, she is not
   going, they are not going. In that case,
   Jane, it sounds like nobody ain't
   going.
7 Now, Susan, can you tell me where
   God lives? Please, Miss, I think He
   lives in the bathroom. In the
   bathroom! Why do you think that?
   Because every morning I can hear my
   father knock on the bathroom door
   and call out God, are you still in
   there?
8 The wife of a naval officer rang one of
   H.M. Dockyards and was addressed
   as Sir by the telephone operator. On
   explaining that she was female, the
   reply came: We call everyone Sir
   here, Madam.
9 I have a Chinese friend who spoke
   only two words of English, Yes and
   No, until he took driving lessons. How
   could that have improved his English?

**'My little brother answered the phone
yesterday, and I called out to him,
"Johnny, who was that on the phone?"
He said it was my boyfriend. Naturally,
I shouted at him and wanted to know
why he had put the phone down. "Well,"
he said, "your boyfriend said it's a long
distance from New York – and I agreed
with him."'**

Well it did, because he now speaks
five English words – Yes, No and Oh,
my God!
10 Employer to gardener: How is your
    wife's pneumonia now? She's still a bit
    weak, Sir, but the peumonia has
    gone. Peumonia? It's pronounced
    neumonia; didn't you hear me say
    neumonia? Yes, Sir, but I didn't like to
    correct you.

**'Excuse me, do you know how to
pronounce "Hawaii"? Is it with a "v"
sound or with a "w"?'
'It's pronounced "Havaii".'
'Thank you.'
'You're velcome.'**

DIRECT AND INDIRECT SPEECH

> **Direct speech gives the exact words somebody spoke.**
> **Reported speech is a narrative version of what was said, and is written after the event.**

Example of <u>direct speech</u> in which quotation marks are used to record actual words spoken:

Two snakes were moving through the jungle. 'Are we poisonous?' asked one snake.
   'Why do you ask?' enquired his friend.
'Because I've just bitten my lip!'

Note the new line every time there is a change of speaker.

Example of <u>reported</u> <u>speech</u> in which quotation marks are not used, because it is a record of what was said and does not have to repeat the exact words.

Two snakes were moving through the jungle, when one snake asked his friend whether they were poisonous. On being asked why, the snake replied that it was because he had just bitten his lip.

Note that a new line for a change of speaker is not required.

There are two main rules to follow when changing direct speech into reported speech (or indirect speech):

   (a)   Change verbs from the present tense to the past tense.
'Why do you ask?' was changed to: On being asked why, . . .
   (b)   Change the pronouns into what is called 'the third person', e.g.
he   him   his   she   her   hers   it   its
they   them   their   theirs
'<u>I've</u> just bitten my lip!' was changed to . . .
<u>he</u> <u>had</u> just bitten . . .

Newspaper reports are usually written in reported speech because it is easier to give an account of the <u>meaning</u> of what has been said rather than the actual words.

A   Write out the following in the form of direct speech.

Mahomet several times called upon the mountain nearby to move and come to him. He then turned to his followers and told them that the mountain was not going to move, and consequently, since the mountain was not going to come to Mahomet, Mahomet was prepared to go to the mountain.

B   Write out the following in the form of reported speech.

'It's always best to do what the mob does,' said Mr Pickwick.
'But suppose there are two mobs?' suggested Mr Snodgrass.
'Shout with the larger mob,' was Mr Pickwick's reply.

The newsagent told me he was out of stock of 'The Sun' and the 'Daily Mirror', and hoped that this would do instead.

THE TIMES
Educational Supplement

C Write out in direct speech what the newsagent told the dog in the picture.

D Write out the following in reported speech.

1 'May I help you, madam?' asked the shop assistant.
'Yes,' said the lady customer, 'I'll take this drinking bowl for my dog.'
'Certainly, madam, but wouldn't you prefer this one, which has "For the Dog" painted on the side?'
'No, thank you,' replied the lady. 'My husband never drinks water, and my dog can't read.'

2 'Why are you two boys so late?' demanded the teacher. 'Don't you know the lesson is half over?'
'We're very sorry, Sir,' said one of the boys, 'but we were so occupied with throwing pebbles into the river, that we just forgot the time.'
 Just then, a boy walked into the classroom, soaking wet, and standing in a pool of water, said, 'Please, Sir, I'm the new boy.'
'What's your name?' asked the teacher.
'Pebbles, Sir.'

E Write out the following in direct speech.

1 A policeman saw a man walking along the street, obviously distressed, and asked the man if he could be of help. The man sobbingly replied that he did not have a friend in the world, and that it was on account of his job. He fed and washed the elephants in a circus. At night he went home smelling like an elephant, and nobody would come near him. The kindly policeman asked if he had ever thought of getting some other kind of job, but the man was most indignant and asked if the policeman was suggesting that he should leave show business.

2 A vicar telephoned his local council to inform them that there was a dead donkey close to the church. The Council official, who thought he was being witty, said that he understood it was the duty of a vicar to bury the dead. The vicar agreed that this was correct, but he considered it was his duty to inform the relatives of the deceased.

3 A customer asked the manager of a shop full of expensive plants, why he had put up a notice 'It is dangerous for children to touch these plants!' The manager replied that it was because he would thump them.

THE SEMI-COLON THAT DOES A BALANCING ACT

| You own a dog | you feed a cat |

> The semi-colon joins together sentences which are closely related and of equal weight.

The semi-colon is a punctuation mark between a comma and a full stop, being closer to the full stop than to the comma. As it does not count as a full stop, the word after a semi-colon does not have a capital letter (unless it is a proper noun).

The semi-colon can help to make a thoughtful, balanced sentence; it is placed between two sentences that deal with the same subject, but are grammatically complete and can stand on their own, e.g.:

1 I took the book back to the shop.
2 There were some pages missing.

I took the book back to the shop; there were some pages missing.

1 Squash and badminton are games for young men.

2 Many older men prefer golf.
Squash and badminton are games for young men; many older men prefer golf.

The semi-colons above suggest a closer connection than the full stop permits. An added advantage is that because the pause is shorter the semi-colon can act as a 'pivot' to balance the two parts of the sentence.

Write out the following, putting in the missing semi-colons.

'Semi' the Seal balances a sentence

1 You can pretend to be serious you cannot pretend to be witty.
2 The noblest of all dogs is the 'hot dog' it feeds the hand that bites it.
3 The stern-faced judge passed sentence the poor defendant passed out.
4 The father read his small son a bedtime story the boy had to wake his father up.
5 Mary got her good looks from her mother she got her quick temper from her father.
6 An acrid smell of burning came from the kitchen as usual the toaster was not working properly.
7 'I washed my hamster in detergent, and it died.'
'Well, I'm not surprised.'
'It wasn't the detergent that killed it I shouldn't have put it in the spin-drier.'
8 The western part of England has mild winters because of the Gulf Stream the eastern part is exposed to cold winds coming from Europe.

THE SEMI-COLON USED FOR CONTRAST

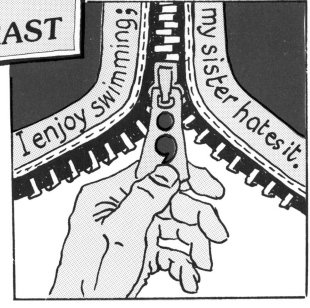

The semi-colon can be used to sharpen a contrast when the two halves of a sentence are similar in structure, but opposite in meaning.

Two separate sentences:
In the classroom, Charles was not too bright. On the sportsfield, he was outstandingly good.

Joined with a semi-colon:
In the classroom, Charles was not too bright; on the sportsfield, he was outstandingly good.

A Write out the following, putting in the missing semi-colons.

1 I enjoy swimming in the cold sea-water my sister can't bear it.
2 An extrovert is a person who never stops talking an introvert is a person who never starts.
3 At his lessons, Jimmy was somewhat slow on the football pitch he was first-rate and very fast.
4 The speaker on the platform was calm and dignified the heckler in the audience was wild and unreasonable.
5 On the surface he seems fairly deep deep down he is very shallow.
6 In good times our friends know us in bad times we know our friends.
7 The young have hopes that never come to pass the old have memories of what never happened.
8 Courage is what it takes to stand up and speak courage is also what it takes to sit down and listen.
9 We can forgive a child who is afraid of the dark the real tragedy is when men are afraid of the light.

Should you wish to group together three statements or ideas, use two semi-colons in one sentence, e.g.

A wise person knows everything; a shrewd person knows everybody; a wise, shrewd person knows everything about everybody.

B Write out the following, putting in the two semi-colons needed.

1 A man who works with his hands is a labourer a man who works with his hands and his brain is a craftsman a man who works with his hands, his brain, and his heart, is an artist.
2 In making a good speech, think up a good beginning then think of a good ending then bring these two as close together as you can.
3 The lights begin to twinkle from the distant houses the long day slowly wanes the pale moon climbs and groups of stars faintly appear.

> **A gossip talks to you about others; a bore talks to you about himself; a brilliant speaker is one who talks to you about you.**

THE SEMI-COLON THAT SETS OUT ITEMS IN A LIST

The big-game hunter on safari has porters to carry the loads, consisting of a tent, (comma) complete with bed and bedding; (semi-colon) cooking and eating utensils; (semi-colon) bottles of beer and lemonade, (comma) and tinned food and preserves; (semi-colon) and sundry other useful items.

> The semi-colon is used to separate items in a list when these are phrases rather than one or two words.

On page 6 (The Comma that Marks off Items in a List) commas acting as porters may be seen carrying small loads. Unfortunately, commas are not strong enough to carry heavy loads such as <u>phrases</u>, and the hunter has had to engage semi-colons to act as safari porters.

The reason for the semi-colon replacing the comma after each item in a list, is that a pause is needed by the reader in order to take in the information. A comma is just not able to provide a sufficiently long pause. For example:

'Bob, what did you think of that beautiful woman at the P.T.A. meeting? I hear she's a wonderful mother to her two well-behaved sons; is a splendid cook; makes all her own dresses; is a marvellous hostess; and is studying for an Open University Degree. She makes me sick!'

Write out the following, putting in all the semi-colons required.

1 A group of cinema engineers listed the following as the ten most dramatic sounds in films: a baby's first cry the blast of a siren the galloping of horses the howl of a dog the sound of a distant train whistle the thunder of breakers on rocks the roar of a forest fire the boom of a ship's foghorn and – most dramatic of all – the wedding march.

2 The most important thing in life is to love someone the second is to have someone loving you the third is to have the first two happening at the same time.

3 The advantages of a bad memory are: one cannot be a good liar one cannot tell long boring stories one forgets unpleasant things and one enjoys places and books a second time round.

4 To get real enjoyment out of a garden, dress in very old clothes hold a spade in one hand hold a cool drink in the other sit back in the hammock and tell your gardener where to dig.

5 Youth is the time to go flashing from one end of the world to the other to try the manners of different nations to see the sunrise in town and country to wait till dawn to hear a few words from a man of wisdom in a far-off land.

THE SEMI-COLON THAT DIVIDES A LIST CONTAINING COMMAS

> **When items in a list contain commas, the semi-colon is used to mark off the main divisions of the sentence.**

In the case of a sentence which contains commas inside the various items or phrases making up the sentence, semi-colons should be used to avoid possible confusion. Here is an example using only commas:

Inigo Jones designed the Banqueting Hall, Whitehall, the Opera House, Covent Garden, the north side of the piazza, Covent Garden, and the garden front of Somerset House.

The confusion can be avoided by replacing the commas at the end of each item, with semi-colons:

Inigo Jones designed the Banqueting Hall, Whitehall; (semi-colon) the Opera House, Covent Garden; (semi-colon) the north side of the piazza, Covent Garden; (semi-colon) and the garden front of Somerset House.

A   Write out the following, putting in the commas and the semi-colons.

1   Following a Communist purge in Poland, this piece of advice was secretly circulated: 'Do not think if you have to think do not talk if you have to talk do not write if you have to write do not sign if you have to sign recant.'

2   There are three wants which can never be satisfied: that of the rich man who wants more wealth that of the sick man who wants his health and that of the old man who wants his youth back.

3   The little girl answered the phone: 'The cat's stuck up in the tree it can't come down the washing-machine has jammed and the floor is flooded the dinner is burning filling the kitchen with smoke the baby is screaming its head off the neighbours are banging on the wall and the canary has escaped or else the cat has eaten it. Can she phone you back?'

4   A restaurant posted this notice on the door: 'As this establishment is temporarily closed for road directions please ask policeman for change go to the bank for water to public fountains matches may be found at hotels public conveniences at your own homes and magazines in dentists' waiting-rooms. Thank you.'

B   The following items are in the wrong order. Write them out correctly, putting in the commas and semi-colons.

1   He coloured it and that was Painting
    He gave mankind the gift of speech and that was Fiction
    He formed it and that was Sculpture
    He peopled it with living beings and that was Drama
    When God thought of the world that was Poetry
    He made the winds and the waves and that was Music

2   genius plus talent is rare and is valuable beyond price
    talent without genius is good but commonplace
    genius without talent is rare but is of little value

THE COLON THAT TAKES THE READER FORWARD

> The colon carries the first part of a sentence forward to the details, speech, or information following.

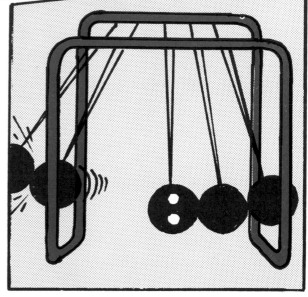

The colon may be used:

(a) as an introduction to speech:
Patient: 'Doctor, I'm invisible!'
Doctor: 'Who said that?'

(b) as an introduction to a quotation, or something written down:
1 Hamlet's main speech begins: 'To be, or not to be . . .'
2 H.M. Prison Notice: 'Haircuts while you wait.'

(c) introduction to a list of items:
'How many ears has Captain Kirk?'
'Three: one left, one right, and a final frontier.'

Note: As it does not count as a full stop, the word after a colon does not have a capital letter (unless it is a proper noun).

Write out the following, putting in all the necessary colons.

1 Boy 'I once discovered a certain cure for amnesia.'
Girl 'What was it?'
Boy 'I can't remember.'
2 Sign displayed in a window 'Free estimates at almost no cost.'
3 Notice on a large green china frog in a photographer's studio 'Some day my prints will come.'
4 We have three kinds of friends those who love us, those who are indifferent to us, and those who hate us.

5 Men join the Foreign Legion for two reasons because they are single, and because they are married.
6 Lazy pupils fall into two categories those who have very little to say and those who have nothing to say.
7 Scrawled on the back of a van 'Make love not war ask driver for full details.'
8 Los Angeles four towns and seventeen suburbs in search of a city.
9 At a market stall selling jars of rejuvenating cream, a woman asked 'Is it really any good?'
'Any good?' echoed the stallholder, and turned to the young girl beside him 'Hand the lady a jar, Mother.'
10 Many of the world's speeches became classics because of one phrase. For example from the speech by Patrick Henry 'Give me liberty, or give me death!'; Abraham Lincoln '. . . government of the people, by the people and for the people'; and from the great speech by Winston Churchill '. . . blood, sweat and tears'.

A second use of the colon is to explain or expand an idea, as in these two examples:

(a) Take care of the minutes: the hours will take care of themselves.

(b) Rich foods are like destiny: they shape our ends.

The colon 'accepts' the first part of the sentence, and 'passes it on' to the second part.

Write out the following, putting in all the necessary colons.

1 Animals are to be envied they know nothing of the evils of this world.

2 Worry is like a rocking-chair it gives you something to do, but gets you nowhere.

3 There are two ways of spreading light to be the candle, or the mirror that reflects it.

4 Self-centred a person who ignores our problems. Busybody one who doesn't.

5 There is only one way to win a nuclear war make certain that it never starts.

6 The most important paragraph in a good story is the first one it contains the seed from which all that follows will grow.

7 Wealth is like sea-water the more we drink, the thirstier we become.

8 This is the final test of a gentleman his respect for those who can be of no possible service to him.

9 Another person's secret is like another person's money you are not as careful with it as you are with your own.

10 Those I like don't have anything in common, but those I love do all of them make me laugh.

11 'I hear you've got yourself a new job but the boss is hard to get on with. Is that true?'
'No, we get on very well he goes his way and I go his.'

12 In rivers, the water that you touch is the last of what has passed and the first of that which comes so with present time.

13 The old believe everything the middle-aged suspect everything the young know everything.

14 A lifetime of happiness no man alive could bear it it would be hell on earth.

15 Every person has three characters the one he shows, the one he has and the one he thinks he has.

16 Red sky at dawning sailors' warning;
Red sky at night sailors' delight.

The doorman threw my coat out of the door: I happened to be in it at the time.

Evening: dream I am marking homework books. Wake up: find I am.

HOW TO CHOOSE BETWEEN THE COLON AND THE SEMI-COLON

SPRINGBOARD CHAMPION

BALANCING CHAMPION

The colon and the semi-colon perform two different tasks in the sentence. The colon is like a springboard: you land on it and are propelled forward. The semi-colon is like the pivot of a see-saw. Example:

Good writing says two things ('springboard' <u>colon</u>): one, which can be explained ('balancing' <u>semi-colon</u>); the other, which cannot.

Write out the following, using colons or semi-colons where required.

1 Definition of a platitude an epigram with a steady job.
2 Wise men talk because they have something to say fools, because they have to say something.
3 To err is human to put the blame on someone else is more so.
4 A pessimist fills in his crossword puzzle with a pencil an optimist uses a ballpoint pen.
5 Whatever you are sure of, be sure of this you are dreadfully like other people.

6 We find it easy to believe that people who praise us are sincere why should anyone lie in telling us the honest truth?
7 We receive three educations one from our parents, one from our teachers, and one from the world the third contradicts the other two.
8 A businessman advertised for a secretary 'Wanted, an assistant who can type one who has no bad habits and is willing to learn.'
9 Holidays are a little like love anticipated with relish experienced with inconvenience remembered with nostalgia.
10 Let me explain how a politician differs from a statesman a politician thinks of the next election a statesman thinks of the next generation.
11 Laziness carries with it two punishments one is failure the other is the success of others.
12 One must not become attached to animals they do not last long enough or to people they last too long.
13 Life resembles the Olympic Games a few men strain their muscles to carry off a prize some bring trinkets to sell to the crowd for a profit the masses just come to see the show.
14 The problem of parents and children at first, children love their parents after a time, they judge them rarely do they forgive them.

'This is your Captain speaking. I have good news, and bad news: (colon) the ship has broken the record to Calais; (semi-colon) your luggage is still at Dover.'

SEMI-COLONS AND COMMAS SHARING A SENTENCE

Sentences containing one or more semi-colons often need commas to make the sentences easier to read and understand.

Example, using semi-colon only:

Power does not corrupt men; fools however if they get into a position of power corrupt power.

Example, with semi-colon and commas:

Power does not corrupt men; fools, however, if they get into a position of power, corrupt power.

A Write out the following, putting in the semi-colons and commas.

1 'Friends Romans countrymen lend me your ears I come to bury Caesar not to praise him.'
2 To the optimist all doors have handles and hinges to the pessimist all doors have locks and latches.
3 A lie is similar to a snowball the longer it is rolled the farther it travels the larger it becomes.
4 The hope of victory in a nuclear war is an illusion if anyone lets the nuclear genie out of the lamp the genie will devour its master too.
5 As long as a word is unspoken you are its master once you utter it you are its slave.
6 'Above her beneath her around her the Machine hummed eternally she did not notice the noise for she had been born with it in her ears.'

7 'There is a tide in the affairs of men which taken at the flood leads on to fortune
Omitted all the voyage of their life is bound in shallows and in miseries.'
8 'It is a far far better thing that I do than I have ever done it is a far far better rest that I go to than I have ever known.'

A style that groups several complete sentences together by the use of semi-colons, because they are closely connected in thought, is far more restful and easy for the reader than the style that leaves him to do the grouping for himself.

B Write out the following, putting in the semi-colons and commas.

1 When you talk to the stupid talk twaddle when you talk to the ignorant brag and boast when you talk to the wise look very humble and ask their opinion.
2 'Ships that pass in the night and speak to each other in passing only a signal shown and a distant voice in the darkness so on the ocean of life we pass and speak to each other only a look and a voice then darkness again and a silence.'

AN INTRODUCTION TO THE PARAGRAPH

> **A paragraph is formed from a group of sentences that have something in common; when put together, they are linked as one part of the stage of an argument, or the unfolding of a story.**

When writing an essay in which you are setting out your views on a certain subject, your opening paragraph serves as an introduction. It is followed by several paragraphs, each of which sets out a point to build up your argument; the essay ends with a final paragraph in the form of a conclusion. Paragraphs are made either by an increase in the line spacing (as in this book) or, more commonly, by 'indenting' – starting the first line further from the margin.

Except for 'Change of Speaker' (see next page) there are no rules about the paragraph; often the subjects of adjoining paragraphs tend to overlap and it is not easy to decide exactly where one should end and the next paragraph begin. The decision must be made, however, because without them, the page becomes a solid block, which is difficult to read. Too many short paragraphs are self-defeating, because the reader has to regroup them in his mind. Paragraphs that are too long make progress difficult for the reader, who is obliged to sort out the ideas and subjects without help from the writer.

The principal benefit of paragraphing is that it gives a clearer and more logical structure to the ideas set out in an essay, and gives a smoother, more coherent flow to the activity and events in a story. The

Paragraphs that are too long make progress difficult for the reader.

secret of writing good paragraphs is separation (dividing the work into units) and continuity (carefully choosing words to begin a paragraph, to ensure that they 'link up' with the previous paragraph).

The art of good paragraphing for an essay is beyond the scope of this book, but the next few pages should help in planning the paragraphs for a story, a letter, or factual writing.

> **Paragraphs carry your ideas forward like the carriages of a railway train, and to ensure that nothing is left behind, they must fit onto one another like automatic couplings.**

NEW PARAGRAPH FOR A CHANGE OF SPEAKER

When writing dialogue, it is essential to begin a new paragraph every time one person begins to speak. This enables the person begins to speak. This enable the reader to know who is speaking. Compare examples A and B:

A   The doctor asked, 'Does it hurt?' 'Only when I laugh.' 'In that case,' he said, 'don't laugh.' 'But I laugh all the time: I'm a circus clown.'

B   The doctor asked, 'Does it hurt?'
    'Only when I laugh.'
    'In that case,' he said, 'don't laugh.'
    'But I laugh all the time: I'm a circus clown.'

Write out the following dialogues, with a new line for change of speaker.

1 'Mummy, I won the nature-study prize.' 'Oh, lovely, Janet. How did you do it?' 'Teacher asked the class how many legs an ostrich has, and I said three.' 'But it has two legs.' 'I was the nearest.'

2 'Does your husband drink?' asked the doctor. 'He takes a drink now and then just to steady himself.' 'And this has no harmful effects?' 'Well, there are times when he gets so steady that he can't move.'

3 'I get these spots in front of my eyes.' The doctor put some drops in his eyes. 'Is that any better?' 'Yes, I can see the spots much clearer now.'

4 In Budapest, a man went to the police station to ask for permission to emigrate to Western Europe. 'Aren't you happy here?' the policeman asked. 'I have no complaints,' said the Hungarian. 'Are you dissatisfied with your work?' 'I have no complaints.' 'Do you have sufficient food?' 'I have no complaints.' 'Are you discontented with the living conditions?' 'I have no complaints.' 'Then why do you want to go to the West?' 'Because there I can have complaints.'

5 'Now that I have become a famous film-star, I have a guilty conscience about my success.' 'Have you done anything about it,' asked the interviewer. 'During my years of poverty, I swore that if I ever got to the top, I would start a foundation to help underprivileged children.' 'What did you do?' 'For years I could do nothing about it. Then came Hollywood and riches.' 'And did you start the foundation?' 'No, I didn't. I said to myself, "The hell with them!"'

NEW PARAGRAPH FOR THE PASSING OF TIME

THE PASSING OF TIME

Do not begin a new paragraph every time you wish to show that time has passed; there would be far too many paragraphs. Do, however, decide when the importance of time passing takes precedence over keeping up the flow of the narrative, and in such cases, begin a new paragraph. The following example has a minor point in which time passes, and one which requires a new paragraph.

Waiting impatiently for the local bus in a small village, I got talking to a man who was passing. We stood chatting for about five minutes while I was giving my opinions on how awful the bus services were these days. He nodded understandingly, then said he must be going, as he was late for work.

A few minutes later, the bus appeared – with him at the wheel.

Write out the following, beginning a new paragraph for every <u>important</u> occasion there is 'passing of time'.

1   I took my radio to a repair shop, explained that there seemed to be something loose inside it, and hurried out to catch a bus. Two weeks later, I went back to the shop. I had not given them my name, so I described the radio and what had been wrong with it. The assistant found my radio. It had a ticket reading: 'Old gentleman – screw loose.'

2   I was a young Merchant Navy officer with an unexpected three hours' shore leave. Having nothing else to do, I decided to join a coach 'mystery tour' at the dock gates. After a short circuit of the local countryside, we returned to the dock gates. We were then given a conducted tour of my own ship.

3   The head doorman at a famous luxury hotel maintains that in his job, honesty is the best policy. Once, as a young man, he forgot to order a car for a wealthy guest. He tried to cover himself by saying that the vehicle had just been struck in the back by another car in Park Lane, but that another car was on its way. He rang the car-hire company, explained his problem, and they promised to send a car at once. Twenty minutes passed and no car. He phoned them again, only to be told that the car they had sent had just been hit in the back by another car in Park Lane.

More exercises on page 52

NEW PARAGRAPH FOR A CHANGE OF PLACE

'I'll let you out on one condition: get me off this island!'

Characters in a story often move from one place to another. Whether or not a new paragraph is required depends upon how much the move affects the development of the story.

As a general rule, the 'change of place' paragraph has priority over paragraphs for 'passing of time', and 'new person'.

In the following example a new paragraph is required, because there is an important change of place from the park to the character's home.

Almost daily, John Smith went for a jog in the park. One morning, a man bumped into him and ran off. John felt for his wallet: it was gone! He set off in hot pursuit, pounced on the fellow and demanded, 'Give me the wallet!' The fellow promptly handed it over.

On returning home, John discovered he had left his own wallet on his desk.

Write out the following, beginning a new paragraph for *every* important change of place.

1 Winter's first fall of snow is a magical event. You go to bed in one world and wake up in another; the very stealth, the eerie quietness of the thing makes it more magical. It flutters down, soundlessly, hour after hour while we are asleep. Outside, a vast transformation is taking place. We know nothing about it, and yet it is as if the house you are in had been dropped down in another continent.

2 We were inexperienced sailors, and thankfully spotting 'MOOR HERE' painted on the sea-wall just above the water-line, we tied the boat up and spent the next few hours in the town. Returning to the harbour, we found that the tide had gone out, leaving our boat stranded on the mud. The receding water now revealed that the words 'MOOR HERE' were followed by 'AT YOUR OWN RISK'.

3 A shipboard conjuror used to do incredible tricks every night, but the ship's parrot always used to shout, 'I know how it's done!' One night, during a performance, the ship hit an iceberg and sank, but the conjuror and the parrot managed to grab a life-raft and get clear. They had been three days on the open sea, when the parrot finally turned to the conjuror and said, 'All right, I give up. How did you do it?'

More exercises on page 53

NEW PARAGRAPH FOR A NEW PERSON

DR. FRANKENSTEIN, D.Sc.

A new paragraph is usually required to introduce a person into a story. In some stories, a character is 'on stage' all the time; in others, he or she may not be referred to for a few paragraphs. When the character returns to the story, a new paragraph is required only if he or she is important to the development of the plot. In the following example, a character (the lady) is merely mentioned in the first paragraph, but merits a new paragraph when she comes back into the story.

A lady hired two workmen to fit her living-room carpet. When they had finished, one noticed a bulge under the middle of the carpet. 'Oh, no,' he said, 'I must have left my cigarettes on the floor. Well, I'm not going to take all that lot up again.' With his hammer, he squashed the lump quite flat.

At that moment, the lady came in with cups of tea, and said, 'Well, you've done a good job, and I've found your cigarettes in the kitchen. By the way, have either of you seen my escaped hamster anywhere?'

Write out the following, beginning a new paragraph where required.

1   A murder trial was well advanced, when one member of the jury revealed that he was completely deaf, and did not have the remotest clue what was happening. The judge asked him if he had heard any evidence at all, and dismissed him when there was no reply. A second juror caused even more excitement when he revealed that he did not speak a word of English. A fluent French speaker, he showed great surprise when told, after two days, that he was hearing a murder trial. The judge ordered a re-trial.

2   Not wishing to attract attention to himself, a bank thief decided to write all his instructions on a piece of paper, rather than shout through the heavy glass windows at the bank. 'This is a hold-up, and I've got a gun!' he wrote, and then held the paper up to be seen. The bemused bank official behind the window waited while he wrote out, 'Put all the money in a paper bag!' This message was pushed through the grille. The cashier read it, and then wrote on the bottom, 'I don't have a paper bag!' and passed it back. The bank thief fled.

More exercises on page 53

THE LAST PARAGRAPH

A story may have a sad ending, or one that is amusing, mysterious or romantic; but whatever ending you decide on, it must be conclusive. Just as the final curtain brings a play to an end, the last paragraph brings a story to an end. In the following examples, the headings explain the reasons for the paragraphs.

1 Introductory paragraph

Jack and Jill grew up, got married and lived by a river so as not to have to climb the hill anymore. Well, things didn't work out as they do in stories, and after a while, they couldn't stand the sight of each other, and split up. Their belongings consisted of a bag of valuable seed-grain, a chicken, and – you could say – the fox that lived close by. The grain had to be protected from the chicken, and the chicken had to be protected from the fox. Jack wanted to keep the chicken, and Jill wanted to keep the grain. So Jill took the grain and rowed to the other bank of the river, and a life of her own.

Important 'passing of time'

Jack was not happy with this state of affairs: he didn't want Jill to have what she wanted. He took his chicken, followed her in his boat, and stole the grain. Jill got into her boat and rowed to Jack's side of the river. She took back her bag of grain, and returned to her own side of the river.

Last paragraph

Jack was not going to take this lying down, and he thought up a brilliant plan. He swam across the river, stole the grain, put it into Jill's boat, and rowed back to his own side in Jill's boat. In the meantime, however, the fox had eaten Jack's chicken.

2 Introductory paragraph

A man is out walking with his son, who tells him a whopping great lie. The father stops, rebukes his son sternly, and tells him that they are approaching Liars' Bridge, which always collapses when a liar tries to cross it. The boy confesses he lied, and they continue their walk.

Important 'change of place' and last paragraph

They arrive at the bridge and start to cross, but the bridge collapses, because the father lied about there being a liars' bridge.

Paragraph exercises on pages 54 and 55

PREPARE TO MEET THE LAST PARAGRAPH

PARAGRAPHS

EXERCISES FOR REVISION

Change of time

Write out the following items in the form of two paragraphs. The second paragraph is required because of an important change of time.

1 A convention of clairvoyants took place at a big hotel. Palm-readers, fortune-tellers and crystal-ball-gazers turned up in large numbers. On the last day, a reporter asked if there would be another conference the following year, and was told that they couldn't see that far ahead.

2 It was rush hour and the tube train was packed, and yet one very fat man was occupying a double seat. For a while, he suffered the disapproving stare of a woman standing near him. Then, with a sigh of resignation, he fished in his pocket and held up two tickets.

3 A Chinese boy saw a three-wise-monkeys figurine for the first time. He was told that the monkey covering its eyes meant 'See no evil', the one covering its ears 'Hear no evil', and the one covering its mouth 'Speak no evil'. After studying them for a minute, he said that it could mean that the one with its hands over its eyes was listening, the one with its hands over its ears was looking, and the one with its hands over its mouth was thinking.

4 A postman on night shift, was collecting the mail from the large post-box in the wall of the building, when a letter appeared through the slot. The next moment, the night was shattered by a girl's startled shriek. Without thinking, the postman had reached up and taken letter out of her hand, with a polite 'thank you'.

5 A man was charged with murder. The chief piece of evidence against him was a hat found near the dead body, which prosecution said belonged to the accused. However, the man's counsel called evidence to show that there were thousands of these hats; it could have belonged to anybody. Eventually, the man was acquitted, and the judge told him that he was discharged. As he seemed reluctant to go, the judge asked him what he was waiting for. The man asked if he could have his hat back.

6 A businessman who arranged to have his body frozen and re-animated years later, invested all his money in growth stock and asked to be frozen till the year 2050. When he thawed out sixty years later, he was given a letter from his brokers telling him the stock was now worth £5 million. Excitedly, he dashed to a public telephone and asked to be connected with the firm immediately. The operator told him to put £1,000 in the slot.

Change of place or person

Write out the following items in the form of two paragraphs. The second paragraph is required, either because of a change of place, or for the introduction of a new person(s).

1 Attempting to catch a persistent thief, the local police set up a secret camera. It was strategically placed in the changing rooms of the sports club where the thefts had been taking place. At the police station the film was played back: they found that all they had managed to film was one of their own men, wandering round in shorts, looking for his stolen clothes.

2 A young lady was trying to teach English to a class of adult foreigners. To begin the lesson, she placed some everyday objects on a table. After asking individuals to hand her the book, the purse, the powder-compact, etc., she turned to an Italian, and asked him to give her the keys. The man looked somewhat surprised, but with a characteristic shrug, he threw his arms round her and kissed her on both cheeks.

3 During the interval of a show, the cast invited a few members of the audience up on the stage to meet them; an eager lady left her seat, walked down the arcade outside and passed through the stage door. She then climbed a flight of dark stairs, and made a right turn. To the great surprise of herself and everyone else, she found herself standing on a brilliantly lit stage, next to actors who looked at her in amazement. She was in the middle of a play being acted at the theatre next door.

'I'm moving to a new paragraph.'

4 Why is it that people always answer the telephone, even at inconvenient moments? Everyone does it. They interrupt conversations and meals; they even let their guests wait, feeling uncomfortable. The person who phones has absolute priority. Why are we so incapable of letting the thing go on ringing? Are we waiting to be told we have won the pools? Is it because there is something in all of us that is ever hopeful? No, the fact of the matter is that – oh, excuse me, the telephone is ringing.

5 A post office sorter once discovered an envelope in the mail addressed to God. He opened it and found a letter from a poor, penniless old lady. She was pleading for divine intervention to help her pay the £96 she owed the Gas Board. Moved to Christian charity, the workers at the post office had a quick whip round and sent the lady £90. By return of post, another letter arrived from her addressed to God. She thanked him profusely for the donation but said that she had received only £90. No doubt, she concluded, the rest of the money had been taken by those thieving post office workers.

PARAGRAPHS

Each of the following items should have four paragraphs; write them out in that form.

1 A hare was continually poking fun at a tortoise because of the slowness of his pace. Although the tortoise tried to ignore him, the day came when the hare challenged the tortoise to a race. A course nearby was set by the animals, and the fox was chosen as judge. He gave a sharp bark and the race was on. In a flash, the hare was out of sight, while the tortoise plodded along at his usual speed. After a time, the hare stopped to wait for the tortoise to come along. The hot sun made him feel drowsy, and he thought he might as well have a quick nap, and finish the race when it was a bit cooler. Meanwhile the tortoise plodded on. He passed the sleeping hare and was almost at the finishing line, when the hare woke up with a start – too far away to save the race. Much ashamed, he crept away while all the animals cheered the winner.

2 Every day, a shepherd boy was sent up the hill to guard a flock of sheep. It was a very lonely spot at the edge of a dark forest, where he spent long, weary hours of watching. One day, to stir up some excitement, he rushed down from the pasture, crying, 'Wolf! Wolf!' The villagers heard the alarm and came running with guns, only to find the sheep grazing peacefully and no wolf in sight. So well had the trick worked, that the foolish boy tried it again and again, and each time, the villagers came running, only to be laughed at for their pains. But there came a day when a wolf really came. The boy screamed and called for help, but all in vain! The villagers, supposing him to be up to his old tricks, paid no attention to his cries, and the wolf devoured the sheep.

3 An old man, stooped by age and hard work, was gathering sticks for his fire in the forest. As he hobbled painfully along, he thought of his troubles and began to feel very sorry for himself. With a hopeless gesture, he threw his bundle of sticks on the ground, and muttered to himself about how hard and miserable his life was, and how he just could not bear it any longer. If only Death would come and take him, he moaned. Even as the words died away in the gloomy forest, Death, in the form of a skeleton in a black robe, stood in front of him. 'I heard you call me, sir,' he said. 'What can I do for you?' 'Please, sir,' replied the old man, 'could you kindly help me put this bundle of sticks back on my shoulder again?'

4 The man at the roulette table was having a run of bad luck, when he heard a ghostly voice in his ear say, 'Number seven!'. He looked furtively around, but nobody was near him. Having nothing to lose, he backed seven, and won. The voice whispered, 'Number seven!', three more times; each time he gambled and won, amassing a fortune. Then the voice said, 'Put everthing on number ten!' He followed the new advice. The croupier spun the wheel – the ball landed on number seven. The mysterious voice in his ear said, 'Damn!'.

Write out the following account of the origin of our alphabet, putting it into paragraph form.

At the time when Joshua and his army were conquering Canaan, writing was a state monopoly in Mesopotamia and Egypt, with only a chosen few, the scribes, ever learning to write. They had to be trained for years by the priesthood, because cuneiform writing (wedge-shaped symbols on clay tablets) and hieroglyphics (picture signs on papyrus) were extremely difficult to master. As Canaan had no organized priesthood, the scribes had to go to other countries for their training; on their return, they would be hired by city officials, army officers and merchants, to write business letters, official documents, schedules and records. The language of Canaan was Semitic, with different dialects spoken wherever different tribes lived; Canaanite, Hebrew and Phoenician were all dialects of the same Semitic language. Between the years 1800 and 1600 B.C., Canaanites working in the turquoise mines, deep in the Sinai desert, borrowed Egyptian hieroglyphics, simplified the signs, and wrote their own language in it. It was an early, but very crude attempt at an alphabet. Between the years 1400 and 1200 B.C., other Semites living on the north Syrian coast opposite the island of Cyprus, in the city of Ugarit, developed a cuneiform alphabet. But our own alphabet was really invented in one of the cities of Canaan between the years 1400 and 1000 B.C., and was perfected by the Canaanites or Phoenicians in the north. The invention of the alphabet was a democratic revolution: from now on, anyone could learn to write.

'Do it again! And this time, use paragraphs!'

Before that time, writing had been clumsy, slow, and very difficult to learn, but now there was no need to memorize hundreds of complicated signs and symbols. The new alphabet had twenty-two letters, all based on the sounds of consonants, with each one named after a familiar object. For example: the Hebrew or Phoenician letter 'A' is aleph, which means 'ox', and the letter A looked roughly like the head of an ox. The letter 'B' was beth, which means 'house', and was originally shaped like a house. The Phoenicians, who were the traders of the ancient world, carried in their ships a cargo more precious than the merchandise – they carried the alphabet. The Greeks adopted it and renamed the letters alpha, beta, gamma, and so on. In Greek, these names have no meaning; they are merely Greek versions of the Semitic aleph, beth, gimel. They did, however, make an important contribution by adding vowels, and passed their alphabet on to the Romans. The Romans changed the shapes of the letters somewhat, and spread the alphabet throughout Europe. That is the story of how we got our alphabet, which we named after the Greek words, alpha beta.

HOW TO WRITE SOCIAL, INFORMAL LETTERS

The informal letter is written to friends or relatives and is usually in a 'conversational' style. Only a few rules apply, as follows:

1 Your own address is put in the top right-hand corner of the page. Each part of the address has a separate line ending in a comma, except the last line, which ends with a full stop. Do not put your name above the address.
2 Leave a little space below the address and write the date.
3 On the left-hand side of the page – a little below the level of the date – write the salutation, for example: 'Dear Jane,'. Note that there is a comma after the salutation.
4 On the next line, begin the letter, indented like a paragraph.
5 Use paragraphs in the usual way.
6 Leave a space below the letter and write the conclusion. This is indented and has a comma after it. On the next line, write your first name. You may make up your own form of conclusion, but the usual ones are: Yours sincerely, Yours affectionately, With best wishes, Kindest regards, Yours with love, See you soon, etc. The first word of the conclusion has a capital letter, but the next word (or next two words) must begin with a small letter.

The Ark,
　Near Mt Ararat,
　Araxes River,
　Armenia.
　31st Jan. 4989 B.C.

Dear Friends,
　The weather is very wet at present, but the forecast is that the rain will stop in forty days.
　Conditions are rather crowded here, but we're making the best of things.
　Wish you were here.
　Regards to all, from
　　the Noah family.

1.　**Brain's Boarding-School,**
　　　The Hollies,
　　　Sandy Lane,
　　　Coventry.

2.　**10th Nov. 1990**

3.　**Dear Mum and Dad,**
4.　**Sorry you couldn't get here for the school play. It was called 'King Lear'. Lots of parents came. Some had seen it before, but they laughed just the same.**
5.　**I'm getting short of cash.**
6.　**Your loving son,**
　　Charlie

HOW TO WRITE SOCIAL, SEMI-FORMAL LETTERS

'Would someone be kind enough to post this letter of resignation for me.'

The semi-formal letter is written to acquaintances, to the editor of a newspaper, to the headmaster of a school, to the secretary of a club, etc. If you know the surname of the person to whom you are writing, use it; if you do not know the name, write 'Dear Sir,' or 'Dear Madam,'. If you do not know whether the person is male or female, use 'Dear Sir or Madam'. The letter is set out in the same way as the informal letter, except that you put the name and address of the person to whom you are writing, just above the salutation. If you do not know the name, write the official position he or she holds, e.g. Headmistress, Manager, Secretary.

For the conclusion of the letter, you could use 'Yours faithfully,'. If, however, you know the name of the person to whom you are writing, or you wish to be slightly less formal, then use 'Yours sincerely,'.

Note that <u>Yours</u> begins with a capital Y, and that the word does <u>not</u> have an apostrophe.

A   Arrange the following, in the form of properly set out semi-formal letters.

1   Flat 4, Woodford Villas, High St., Birmingham. To: Miss M. Jones, Cannonball Comprehensive School, Hollybush Hill, Birmingham, CV3 8NB. 30th Nov. 1986. Dear Miss Jones, Kindly excuse Robert's absence yesterday, as he fell into the mud on his way to school. By doing the same, you will oblige, Yours truly, Ethel Smith (Mrs)

The Chieftain's Hut,
Jungle Village,
Alo-ngwa-yaw-ay.

1st Sept. 1855

The Bishop of Birmancastle,
Birmancastle Cathedral,
England.

Your Grace,
    Please find enclosed a letter of resignation from our missionary.
    He was a wonderful spiritual guide; we found him to be kind, considerate, and delicious.
    Yours truly,
    Mbingo (Cannibal Chief)

---

2   7 Tiptree Road, Eccles Estate, Glasgow, E16 2JD Santa Claus, North Pole. 10th Dec. 1986. Dear Santa Claus, Last year I got a sister instead of a bike. Maybe some other boy wanted a sister and got my bike. We have kept the sister, but I would still like a bike. Yours sincerely, Billy McDuff

B   Arrange the following similarly, but you will have to supply all the addresses and dates.

1   Dear Parents, Please study the enclosed list of birthdays, and let me know if your child's name is missing. Yours truly, Arthur Davies (Headmaster) Dear Mr Davies, As requested, I am writing to let you know that my child's name is Missing. Yours sincerely, Janice Missing (Mrs)

HOW TO WRITE FORMAL AND BUSINESS LETTERS

'It's my latest invention; I'm going to call it a "letter". If it sells well, I shall call it a "business letter".'

The formal letter is written to a person in his or her official capacity. For example, a formal letter would be sent to the manager of a shop, if you wished to complain about faulty goods bought there.

For the formal or business letter, use the salutation 'Dear Sir,' or 'Dear Madam,' (note capital S and M).

Use 'Dear Sir,' if you do not know whether the person is male or female.

When writing the address, if you do not know whether 'Mrs' or 'Miss' is correct, you may use 'Ms' (note no full stop). Unless you happen to know the person addressed, use the conclusion 'Yours faithfully,'. Sign the letter legibly with your full name, but do not add 'Mr' or 'Miss'.

It is usual in business correspondence, for the addresses to be set out in 'block form' without any punctuation, and for paragraphs to be spaced instead of indented. An example of this style is shown in the next column.

THE ACME MANUFACTURING COMPANY

Ref CR/SB24
1st Sept. 90

Unit 12
Industrial Estate
Netherhall
Newtown CV3 2LG

The Personnel Manager
Top Products Co. Ltd
10–15 High St
Newtown PG1 4AX

Dear Sir

We thank you for your letter of the 28th August requesting a reference for Mr John Smith, who worked for us recently.

We are pleased to say that John is an honest and likeable young man, and anybody who can get John to work for him will be very lucky.

Yours faithfully
Charles Roberts
Managing Director

'It sometimes happens that the person who dictates a letter is not available for signature, and it is signed on the person's behalf, for example:

Yours faithfully
p.p. Charles Roberts
Bill Robinson

Any reply should be sent to Mr Roberts and not to Mr Robinson and if there has been a reference given, mention it in your reply.

HOW TO WRITE A LETTER APPLYING FOR A JOB

'It's for you, Robin. It's a letter of application from the Sheriff – he wants to join our merry band.'

Always keep a carbon copy (or make a photocopy) of a formal or business letter. The copy will provide a record of the address of the person to whom you are writing, and it can always be referred to as a reminder.

Perhaps the most important letter you will need to write is the letter of application for a job. As you will want to make a good impression, the following points may be useful.

1 Paper and envelope should be white, of good quality, and reasonably large. A good paper size is A4 (8¼″ by 11¾″) and the envelope to fit A4 is 4¼″ by 8½″.
2 Employers prefer to receive a typewritten letter as it is easier to read, but the signature must be handwritten.
3 If the letter is to be written, make sure your handwriting is not too small, and is clear, well-spaced and easy to read.
4 Make a rough draft (or more than one draft) before writing the finished letter, and check it carefully for errors or omissions. Pay particular attention to spelling and punctuation.
5 Do not have mistakes crossed out; it is better to scrap the letter and start again.
6 Set the letter out so that it is centrally placed on the page, with a wide border on both left and right.
7 Fold the letter so that it fits the envelope perfectly.

Paragraphs in a letter are just as important as in an essay or story. A letter of application should have three or four paragraphs, for example:

1 State how you know about the vacancy (through an advertisement, an agency, from another person, etc.) and refer to the particular job by name.
2 Give your age and general qualifications, such as examination results, prizes won, and any special achievements that are relevant. Give details of your education.
3 State your specific reason for claiming to be able to do the job. Refer to testimonial, references, or persons who could vouch for you.
4 Make a request for an interview, at which you would be pleased to answer any questions about your suitability for the job.

Write a few letters of application for imaginary jobs you would like to have, and for which you think you would be suitable. Write in the date, and make up appropriate names and addresses.

JUST FOR FUN!

1 An order was placed for a road sign to be painted, but unfortunately it was dictated over the phone, and the punctuation went wrong. Write out a corrected sign to replace the faulty one below.

THIS ENTRANCE IS IN USE BY CONTRACTORS' CHILDREN, AND THE PUBLIC ARE WARNED NOT TO USE IT.

2 The following sixteen people have a special way of saying 'Good morning!' to each other. Match the greeting with the person, and supply the missing punctuation. The first one is done for you:

The doctor said, 'How are you today?'

DOCTOR   hows tricks
TEACHER   hi down there
OPTICIAN   all right thats the ticket
MAGICIAN   springs in the air
UNDERTAKER   what a heavenly blue sky
DITCH-DIGGER   what do you know
ARCHEOLOGIST   nice to see you looking well
WATCHMAKER   its a fare old day
STEEPLEJACK   how are you today
INVENTOR   itll be a fine day i think
BUS CONDUCTOR   hi up there
MARATHON RUNNER   anything new turned up
TRAFFIC-WARDEN   heard anything useful
CLERGYMAN   any plans for today
FORECASTER   im just jogging along
ARCHITECT   have a good mourning

3 Write out the following, complete with full punctuation and paragraphs.

one day in the jungle there was a football match between the elephants and the insects by half time the elephants were winning 39–0 then in the second half a centipede came on to play for the insects he was a brilliant player the elephants could find no way to stop him and by the end of the match the score was 46–39 to the insects as they were leaving the field the captain of the elephants said what puzzles me is why didnt you play that centipede in the first half we would have said the captain of the insects the only trouble is it takes him an hour to get his boots on

4 Write out the following graffiti, with suitable punctuation:

(a) schizophrenia divides and rules ok
(b) the marquess of queensbury rules ko
(c) james bond rules ook
(d) prof einstein rules relatively ok
(e) in spain the rules are ole
(f) gude sppeling rools owkai

5 Write out the following putting in the missing letters in the underlined words, and supplying the punctuation.

Emerging from the ma__e we saw the ma__e warrior seated on a grey ma__e with a flowing ma__e his dutiful ma__e carrying the warriors heavy ma__e rode behind him on a pony they ma__e a brave picture in the sunlight

6 The following was written on a typewriter with a faulty space-bar. Write it out correctly, complete with punctuation.

al lou rliv eswea recru she dbyt hew eig hto fwo rdsw eha vet obui ldupar easo nab levoca bular ymas terth espe lli ngan dlea rnho wtow ritei nwel lpun ctu at edsen tenc esth ewho lethin ghas mel ostfo rwo rdse xce pttos aytha tthi sis

THEEND